JANF   CANBY PUBLIC LIBRARY   SP
           292 N. HOLLY
        CANBY, OR

D0789640

Book of Poems
(Selection)

Libro de poemas
(selección)

A Dual-Language Book

Federico García Lorca

Edited and Translated by
STANLEY APPELBAUM

DOVER PUBLICATIONS, INC.
Mineola, New York

Copyright

Selection, English translation, Introduction, and footnotes copyright © 2004 by
Dover Publications, Inc.
All rights reserved.

Bibliographical Note

This Dover edition, first published in 2004, includes the complete Spanish text of
fifty-five poems from *Libro de poemas* (Maroto, Madrid, 1921). The selection was
made by Stanley Appelbaum, who also provided the new English translations, the
Introduction, and the footnotes.

Library of Congress Cataloging-in-Publication Data

García Lorca, Federico, 1898–1936.
    [Libro de poemas. Spanish & English. Selections]
    Books of poems : (selection) = Libro de poemas : (selección) / Federico García
Lorca ; edited and translated by Stanley Appelbaum.
    p. cm. — (A Dual-language book)
    "This Dover edition [. . .] includes the complete Spanish text of fifty-five poems
from Libro de Poemas (Maroto, Madrid, 1921)"—T.p. verso.
    Includes index.
    ISBN 0-486-43650-0 (pbk.)
    1. García Lorca, Federico, 1898–1936—Translations into English. I. Title: Libro
de poemas. II. Appelbaum, Stanley. III. Title. IV. Series.

PQ6613.A763A2115 2004
861'.62—dc22

2004052893

Manufactured in the United States of America
Dover Publications, Inc., 31 East 2nd Street, Mineola, N.Y. 11501

CONTENTS

iii

INTRODUCTION

Lorca

The most widely translated Spanish author, surpassed only by
Cervantes in the amount of critical commentary devoted to him, is
Federico García Lorca.[1] Though his already popular works are a suf-
ficient foundation for anyone's fame, successive editions of so-called
Complete Works publications continue to add more juvenilia, frag-
ments, and other hitherto unpublished items, some of which still ap-
pear only in altogether separate compilations; not many occasional
readers are aware of the full scope of his output, and many treasures
await universal recognition.

Lorca was born in 1898 into a talented family residing in an unusu-
ally liberal and culturally alert village, Fuente Vaqueros, just a few
miles west of Granada in the fertile plain called the Vega. Fortunately
his father had become quite wealthy growing sugar beets, because
Federico had to be subsidized by his father for almost all of his short
life, achieving financial independence very late. In 1907 the family
moved to another village, Vega de Zujaira (both villages, along with
Granada and Madrid, are cited in *Libro de poemas* as places where in-
dividual poems were written).

In 1909 the family moved to the city of Granada, where Federico
attended secondary school (which he had begun the previous year in
somewhat distant Almería). He also took piano and guitar lessons;
later he was to be a good pianist and enough of a composer to har-
monize local folk songs. In addition, he had a talent for drawing; his
mature works, very linear, are reminiscent of similar cartoonlike
pieces by Cocteau and Dalí.

In 1915 Lorca entered Granada University, taking courses in law
and in "philosophy-and-letters"; though highly gifted, he was a lazy

---

1. García, his father's family name, is his true surname, but when the father's name
is as commonly found as García is, a more distinctive mother's family name, in this case
Lorca, is often used as a handy one-word identification.

student, but his exuberance and charm (despite a morbid fear of death, related to childhood experiences) made him many lasting friendships, some of which were to smooth his way in Madrid. It was probably around this time, too, that he began to write poetry. In 1917 he had his first article published: prophetically, a fantasy dialogue about Granada. He was constantly sketching plays, both whimsical and more realistic, and writing brief prose poems and other prose pieces; these early works already reflect subject matter and themes that were to preoccupy him all his life.

The result of university-sponsored group trips all around Spain in 1916 and 1917 was his first book, in 1918, the prose *Impresiones y paisajes* (Impressions and Landscapes); one of the three local people who persuaded his father to finance the printing was the guitarist Andrés Segovia. (The book sold poorly and Federico soon withdrew it.)

In 1919 Lorca moved to Madrid, which he had visited briefly the year before, making valuable contacts. Now he went to live in the prestigious Residencia de Estudiantes (Students' Hostel), where he renewed older Granada friendships and met many celebrities and future celebrities from other parts of Spain. (With a few interruptions, he lived in the Residencia during semesters until 1928.) Meanwhile, his assiduity at studies hadn't increased, and his father exerted a great deal of pressure, urging him to "succeed" in a recognizable profession. Federico's younger brother Francisco (Paquito) was a model student and an achiever, but Federico never resented the implied "competition." Eventually, almost as an afterthought, he took a law degree in 1923.

His first play to be produced was *El maleficio de la mariposa* (The Butterfly's Evil Spell; Madrid, 1920). Though it was performed under the most favorable auspices (the director was the eminent playwright Gregorio Martínez Sierra, and the role of the butterfly was danced by the great La Argentinita), it was a dismal failure; audiences of the day didn't warm to this story about a young cockroach-poet who dies because he can never win the love of the gorgeous butterfly. Nevertheless, this verse play is highly readable, and many of its features prefigure later work. Particularly, some of the poems in *Libro de poemas* (pieces written between 1918 and 1920) are very close to *Mariposa* material. La Argentinita, whose real name was Encarnación López Júlvez, was to come back into Lorca's life time and again; in 1931 they made a series of recordings of folk songs he had harmonized, with her singing and him at the piano. (Also, between 1920 and 1923 Lorca was writing the poems which he collected into *Suites*, never published in his lifetime.)

In 1921 he published the above-mentioned *Libro de poemas*, his first (and longest) volume of verse, the source of the 55 poems reprinted and translated in their entirety in this Dover volume. The second section of this Introduction discusses the *Libro de poemas* at some length.

In 1919, Lorca had met the eminent Andalusian composer Manuel de Falla, with whom he was now, in 1922, associated in a flamenco (strictly speaking, *cante jondo*) festival in Granada. In 1923 they also staged one of Lorca's inventive puppet plays together. All through the early 1920s Federico was getting ideas for, and slowly writing, a good number of poems and plays that were not to see the light for some time. The plays were generally held back for lack of a producer; the poems, because Lorca was reluctant to share them with the world (one of his greatest delights was to recite them, very dramatically, to small groups of appreciative friends; at most, he might include an as-yet unpublished poem in one of his frequent lectures). As a result of these delays, for several years none of his poem volumes or theatrical premieres contained brand-new product, and he himself habitually expressed dissatisfaction at the material, as representing a stage in his development which he had already passed by.[2]

In 1923, at the Residencia, Lorca met the great love of his life, the artist Salvador Dalí. They enjoyed each other's company frequently for the next few years, and images of Lorca appear in a number of Dalí's works from that era. If they never had sex together, it wasn't for want of encouragement on the part of Lorca, who was decidedly ho-mosexual and had a number of male bedfellows over the years, though he wasn't promiscuous and he tried to establish lasting relationships. He wrote a major ode to Dalí in 1925 (published 1926).

The year 1927 was one of major importance for Federico. Many of his pieces were published in periodicals. He had an exhibition of drawings in Barcelona (thanks to the influence Dalí was able to exert in his native Catalonia). His play *Mariana Pineda*, about a historical "Betsy Ross" from Granada martyred because she embroidered a flag for rebels who *lost*, premiered successfully in both Barcelona and Madrid. (This play, with its strong reminiscence of the Scarpia-vs.-Tosca element in Sardou's play and Puccini's opera, is a good example of the melodrama which was to make Lorca's later rural-Andalusian prose plays so powerful and so popular.) A volume of lyric poems

2. This nervousness, which even led him to concur with the captiousness of reviewers of the *Libro de poemas*, shouldn't be taken to mean that he was really disavowing his work.

written between 1921 and 1924 was published with the title *Canciones* (Songs). And lastly, he participated in the tercentary-of-death celebrations that rehabilitated the sublime Baroque poet Luis de Góngora, and that helped give the "generation of 1927" (writers of approximately the same age as Lorca) its sobriquet. The trip for seven from Madrid to Andalusia for the Góngora hommage was financed by a torero of high culture, with many literary friends, Ignacio Sánchez Mejías, who, incidentally, in this same year of 1927, became the lover of Lorca's old friend La Argentinita.

In 1928 Federico became the cofounder and the copublisher of both issues of the avant-garde magazine *gallo* (rooster). In the same year, he published the thrilling *Romancero gitano* (Gypsy Ballads), deservedly his most popular work. These poems, reviving the form and technique of Spanish medieval and Renaissance narrative ballads, had been written between 1923 and 1927.

An old acquaintance of Lorca's, the Granada law professor Fernando de los Ríos, an ardent socialist (and anathema to the dictator then governing Spain, Miguel Primo de Rivera), was now invited to lecture at Columbia University in New York. Lorca accepted his invitation to go along and enroll as a graduate student. He let it be known that he was trying to become more cosmopolitan, but he may have actually been escaping, both from his father's pressure (his successes hadn't been lucrative) and from romantic disappointments. For one thing, Luis Buñuel (the future great filmmaker) had estranged Dalí from him, luring the Catalan to Paris, and Lorca was convinced that the (now famous) short experimental film the two had made together in 1928, *Un chien andalou* (An Andalusian Dog), specifically targeted him and held him up to ridicule.

Lorca was in the New World from June 1929 to June 1930, spending some of the time in Vermont and the last three months in Cuba. The bitter Expressionistic or Surrealistic poems inspired in him by the metropolis weren't published until after his death—*Poeta en Nueva York* (The Poet in New York), Mexico, 1940 (except for the "Oda a Walt Whitman," which was published in Mexico in 1934 in an edition of fifty copies). The Harlem poems in *Poeta,* like Lorca's earlier poems about downtrodden Gypsies, seem to stem from a well-to-do young man's guilt feelings about impoverished and marginalized minorities, but the unmistakably heartfelt tones may stem from Lorca's very real "outsider" status as a gay in the prim, *macho* Spain of his day.

At the very end of the year 1930, Lorca's play *La zapatera prodigiosa* (The Shoemaker's Prodigious Wife) had its premiere in Madrid.

But he was never able to achieve a production of the highly experimental, often openly homosexual play he had written in Cuba, *El público* (The Audience; generally nontranslated as *The Public*). It has been suggested that he undertook his rural Andalusian tragedies (his greatest theatrical successes) as a relatively safe bet, in view of the brick wall *El público* had run up against.

In 1931 he published the *Poema del cante jondo* (Poem of Cante Jondo), written in 1921 and 1922. The same year also witnessed the beginning of the Second Spanish Republic. While Fernando de los Ríos, Federico's old friend and mentor, was minister of education, he pushed through a scheme for a mobile theater to tour the provinces, bringing culture to the masses. Lorca was recruited as one of two directors in 1932. From then until 1935, with increasingly long interruptions when his personal projects finally took off and occupied more of his time, he was associated with La Barraca (The Cabin), as this student theater was called, directing and adapting (sometimes with huge tendentious cuts) Spanish classic plays.

Madrid in 1933 was the site of the premieres of two plays: the fanciful tragicomedy *Amor de don Perlimpín con Belisa en su jardín* (The Romance of Don Perlimpín and Belisa in His Garden; generally referred to in English as *Don Perlimpín*) and the enormously successful *Bodas de sangre* (Blood Wedding), the work that finally began to earn real money for its author. That same year, in Barcelona, an expanded version of *La zapatera prodigiosa* was staged. Oddly enough, it was at this time that Federico decided to move in with his parents again (they were now in Madrid). Before the year was over, Lorca had also made an absolutely triumphant journey to Buenos Aires, where he directed his plays and gave lectures.

The year 1934 was signalized by the highly successful premiere of *Yerma* in Madrid. Also in that year, Lorca's friend and patron Ignacio Sánchez Mejías was gored in the bullring and died because of inadequate medical attention. Lorca's stirring ode, *Llanto por Ignacio Sánchez Mejías* (often known in English as *Lament for the Death of a Bullfighter*), was published in 1935, with a dedication to La Argentinita. Also in 1935: a minor off-Broadway production of *Blood Wedding* in English in New York; the premiere in Barcelona of *Doña Rosita la soltera; o Lenguaje de las flores* (Doña Rosita the Spinster; or, Language of Flowers); and the publication of *Primeras canciones* (First Songs), poems written in 1922.

In 1936, *Bodas de sangre* was published. Lorca was planning a trip to Mexico, to direct his plays there as he had done in Argentina. He

gave a reading of his play *La casa de Bernarda Alba* (The House of
Bernarda Alba), and put into rehearsal his highly experimental, almost
hermetic play *Así que pasen cinco años* (translated as *When Five Years
Pass;* the meaning is more like "just as soon as five years have gone
by"). But public events caught up with him. Strong rumors of a coup
being prepared against the Republic made him panicky. Though he
was advised he'd be safer in Madrid, and much safer in France, his
temperament led him to return to the womb, to Granada, where his
parents had recently taken up residence again.

Lorca reached Granada only days before Franco's coup actually oc-
curred in mid-July. By July 23, Granada, through the mutiny of its gar-
rison, was in anti-Republican hands, and a reign of terror (fueled, as
always in Spain, by personal vendettas) began. Lorca was harassed as
a perceived atheist, a vocal anti-fascist, and a despised homosexual.
Placed under house arrest for no cogent reason, he foolishly broke it
and hid in a friend's house, where he was readily ferreted out.
Arrested, he was shot, out in the countryside, with numerous other
political victims, on August 19, becoming a martyr to the Republican
cause and a permanent embarrassment to Franco.

Both his plays and his poetry are imbued with Andalusian folklore
(often, children's rhymes), which inspires and structures entire large
works, as well as significant details. As a playwright, he was greatly in-
debted to the avant-garde plays of Ramón del Valle-Inclán
(1866–1936). As a poet, he was greatly influenced early on by *mod-
ernismo* (a synthesis of French Symbolism and Parnassianism), as in-
troduced to Spain by the Nicaraguan Rubén Darío around the time of
Lorca's birth, and as later modified and made quieter and subtler by
another Andalusian, Juan Ramón Jiménez. As Lorca matured, how-
ever, it was his own genius that gave his best work its unmistakable
stamp of passionate excitement and thoroughly poetical thought.

The *Libro de poemas*

The *Libro de poemas,* Lorca's first volume of verse (but not his earli-
est efforts!) was published in Madrid in 1921 by "Imprenta Maroto";
Gabriel García Maroto, the (vanity) publisher, was a painter by pro-
fession. Six of the poems had been printed earlier: "Madrigal" (the
one beginning "Mi beso"), "Encrucijada," and "La sombra de mi
alma" first appeared in the December 11, 1920 issue (No. 293) of
España (Madrid); "Veleta," "Deseo," and "Sueño" (the one beginning

"Mi corazón") were first published in the January 1921 number (II, 8) of *La Pluma* (Madrid).

No editor doubts that the dates assigned by Lorca to all the poems but one (dates ranging between 1918 and 1920) are really those of their composition. The only poem not dated in its heading is "Camino," which from many indications seems to have been added in proofs into a very tight space, without enough room for a date (the manner of its appearance in the 1921 volume misled some later editors into thinking it was a continuation of the preceding poem); because of the time of its insertion, "Camino" may very well date from 1921, thus being the most recent item in the book.

Assuming (safely) that "Camino" is a separate poem, there are 68 altogether in the 1921 first edition: 12 dated 1918, 26 dated 1919, and 29 dated 1920, plus "Camino." Of this total, the present Dover volume includes 55, omitting 4 from 1918, 2 from 1919, and 7 from 1920; the ones selected appear in their entirety and in their original sequence, and include the opening and closing poems of the 1921 volume.[3] Later editions of *Libro de poemas* (usually in "complete-works" editions) vary in punctuation, line and stanza breaks, and very occasionally in wording; the form of the Dover selection is much like that of 1921, merely making the emendations of typos that all editors agree on.

Libro de poemas, in the eyes of one major historian of literature, has the most complex spiritual content of any of Lorca's volumes. Another preeminent critic states that Lorca, in this volume, was still finding his own voice, and that he had not yet mastered all the means eventually at his disposal, but that nevertheless the *Libro de poemas* goes well beyond a mere promise of greater things to come, and includes many highly successful poems. In fact, Lorca is already a master of technique (which he always considered as important as content), making dashing use of a number of traditional meters and stanza forms, assonance, and pure rhyme, as well as introducing bold innovations. For one thing, he is already employing repeated refrains based on Spanish folklore and lyric verse of the Golden Age and earlier, and he is beginning to renovate such forms as the *romance* (the traditional, assonating narrative ballad) and the *serranilla* (lyrics depicting encounters between amorous noblemen and self-respecting country girls). Some of the pieces in *Libro de poemas* are heartfelt and

---

3. Dover Publications specifically requested that a selection be made. The 13 poems omitted appeared to the translator/editor to be more rhetorical, cerebral, ordinary, or flippant than the rest, or too closely tied to current events; none is particularly long.

flawless, and are surpassed only by the poet's own later work, which can be more intense and searing, and even bolder in conception.

In the *Libro de poemas*, Lorca was only marginally influenced by such trends of the moment as ultraism, creationism, and futurism, which tended to be artificially galvanic, exalting machinery and material "progress." He was already earthy, playful, and solemn in turns, appreciative of the Andalusian countryside and of nature in general, and already concerned with his personal emotional preoccupations, particularly death, with which he frequently associates a coldly metallic, oddly unfriendly moon. Above all, he was already a master of metaphor, not merely locally applied for coloration, but fundamental to an entire poem, underlying it as well as ramifying into brilliantly inventive offshoots. Symbols he would use throughout his oeuvre are already present: the weather vane, the rose, the iris.

Just as he consciously avoided milking the fad, very popular in those days, of tinselly Moorish Andalusianism, so he makes no use of local dialect or any oddities of syntax, apart from one or two nonstandard verb forms. The few unusual words he employs are generally of his own coinage, but readily understandable. (The forms *pentágrama* and *metamórfosis*, historically correct, were still permissible at the time; nowadays they are written without accent marks, and are stressed on the next-to-last syllable.)

The 1921 edition contained the following "Words in Justification," which most editors believe are by Lorca himself, though some are convinced they were added by his publisher Maroto:

"In this book, which is all youthful ardor, torture, and measureless ambition, I offer the true image of my days of adolescence and young manhood, those days which connect the present moment to my own not-too-distant childhood.

"These disordered[4] pages are a faithful reflection of my heart and mind, tinged with the coloring that would be lent to them, if it possessed it, by the throbbing life all around which has only recently opened up to my sight.

"The birth of each one of these poems that you hold in your hand, reader, is akin to the sprouting of a new shoot on the lyrical tree of my flowering life. It would be an act of vileness to belittle this work, which is so closely entwined with my own life.

"Despite its formal flaws, despite its undoubted limitations, this

---

4. Some critics have taken this word to mean that the sequence of poems was not determined by Lorca, or that, if it was, he was dissatisfied with it.

book will have the power, among many others that I find in it, of reminding me at every moment about my passionate childhood, which traipsed about, nude, in the meadows of a fertile plain against the backdrop of a mountain range." The entire 1921 volume was dedicated: "To my brother Paquito." Among the dedicatees of individual poems are the following: Adolfo Salazar was an eminent composer and critic; the poem dedicated to him is of particularly musical interest. Emilio Prados was a poet, a friend of Lorca's at the Residencia de Estudiantes, and (later) the publisher of his volume *Canciones* (in 1927). Melchor Fernández Almagro was a Granada friend who had reached Madrid before Lorca, as was José Mora Guarnido, later a journalist and author of an important biography of Lorca in 1958. Manuel Ángeles Ortiz was a painter who later worked in Picasso's studio in Paris. "María Luisa" may very well be María Luisa Egea González, whom Lorca had a crush on in 1917; she was in Madrid by 1918; another early poem by Lorca is dedicated to her. Pepe Cienfuegos (Pepe is normally a pet name for José) was perhaps a relative of the Granadan poet Alberto Álvarez de Cienfuegos (or even Alberto himself with an unusual nickname).

The poems in *Libro de poemas* have no need of elucidation or interpretation, but a few comments are in order:

"Los encuentros de un caracol aventurero" is concerned with humble small creatures, like the 1920 play *El maleficio de la mariposa* (in which most of the characters are roaches and grubs). The poem reflects the youthful author's rebellion against social norms and his questioning of traditional religion.

"Elegía a Doña Juana la Loca" is addressed to Juana (Joanna, Joan; 1479–1555), daughter of the "Catholic monarchs" Ferdinand and Isabella (Fernando II of Aragon and V of Castile, and Isabel I of Castile [and León]). When her mother died in 1504, Juana became queen of Castile, her father retaining Aragon (and control over her). When her husband, Philip the Handsome (son of Holy Roman Emperor Maximilian I), died in 1506, Juana's latent insanity worsened and she could no longer rule. Some pious, patriotic Spaniards believe that Juana, her parents, and her husband are still buried in the Royal Chapel of Granada Cathedral (where they have funerary monuments), even though the ravages of Napoleonic troops in 1812 caused irreparable confusion in the gravesites. "Dauro" is a rare alternative Arabic name for the Darro, the river that runs through (and now largely under) Granada. In this poem Lorca is using a traditional lofty

style, which occurs in some other early poems, but which he later de-
cided not to pursue.

"Elegía" is a magnificent tribute to a woman whose chance for love
and motherhood has been wasted. It is a worthy forerunner of later
works with analogous themes: *Yerma, Doña Rosita la soltera,* and *La
casa de Bernarda Alba.*

"Santiago" is, of course, Saint James the Apostle, patron saint of
Spain and martial killer of Moors, his remains traditionally believed to
rest in Santiago de Compostela, Galicia.

"El diamante" occurs in more different versions—four—than any
other poem in the *Libro de poemas.* Besides the version in the 1921
volume, there is an early manuscript (in which it is entitled "Lección"
[Lesson]), and two versions from the early 1930s, one in the hand-
written manuscript and the other in the typescript of one of Lorca's
lectures; he had revised the poem to show a new approach to the *ro-
mance* form, and there is no indication that he wished to revise the
Libro de poemas any further. (Unlike Juan Ramón Jiménez, for ex-
ample, who was constantly rewriting already published material,
Lorca was always impatiently looking ahead.)

"Balada de un día de julio" is a dialogue reminiscent of Renaissance
serranillas (see above). The *viudita* jingle (from little girls' round
games) is also used prominently in an early melodramatic play never
published by Lorca, *La viudita que se quería casar* (The Little Widow
Who Wanted to Marry; 1919–1920).

"Tarde" shows the strongest Rubén Darío influence, the opening
line being a striking reminiscence of Rubén's poem "Sinfonía en gris
mayor" (Symphony in Gray Major).

"Prólogo" (like a couple of other items in the *Libro de poemas*)
shows the influence of French nineteenth-century Satanism, as ex-
emplified by Baudelaire and others. In this poem, Lorca identifies
himself with the hero of Goethe's *Faust.* The cry "Heinrich!
Heinrich!" (Faust's Christian name), uttered by a receding voice, to
be identified with that of Margarete (Gretchen) as she is whisked
away to heaven, closes Part One of Goethe's work.

"Aire de nocturno" has a recurring refrain which Lorca reused, in
an adapted form, in his play *Así que pasen cinco años* (completed in
1931).

The present Dover translation is line-for-line and literal, making no
attempt at meter, rhyme, or assonance; any euphony it may possess is
a secondary phenomenon.

Book of Poems
(Selection)

Libro de poemas
(selección)

Veleta

Julio de 1920

(Fuente Vaqueros, Granada)

Viento del Sur.
Moreno, ardiente,
llegas sobre mi carne,
trayéndome semilla
de brillantes
miradas, empapado
de azahares.

Pones roja la luna
y sollozantes
los álamos cautivos, pero vienes
¡demasiado tarde!
¡Ya he enrollado la noche de mi cuento
en el estante!

Sin ningún viento,
¡hazme caso!
Gira, corazón;
gira, corazón.

Aire del Norte,
¡oso blanco del viento!,
llegas sobre mi carne
tembloroso de auroras
boreales,
con tu capa de espectros
capitanes,
y riyéndote a gritos
del Dante.
¡Oh pulidor de estrellas!
Pero vienes
demasiado tarde.

Weather Vane

July 1920

(Fuente Vaqueros, Granada)

South wind.
Swarthy, ardent,
you blow upon my skin,
bringing me the seed
of flashing
glances, steeped as you are
in orange blossom.

You turn the moon red
and cause the captive
poplars to sob, but you come
too late!
I have already rolled up the night of my tale
on the shelf!

Without any wind,
pay heed to me!
Spin around, my heart;
spin around, my heart.

Air from the North,
the wind's polar bear!
You blow on my skin,
trembling as you are with the aurora
borealis,
with your cape of spectral
captains,
laughing loudly
at Dante.
O polisher of stars!
But you come
too late.

Mi almario está musgoso
y he perdido la llave.
  Sin ningún viento,
  ¡hazme caso!
  Gira, corazón;
  gira, corazón.

  Brisas, gnomos y vientos
de ninguna parte,
mosquitos de la rosa
de pétalos pirámides,
alisios destetados
entre los rudos árboles,
flautas en la tormenta,
¡dejadme!
Tiene recias cadenas
mi recuerdo,
y está cautiva el ave
que dibuja con trinos
la tarde.

  Las cosas que se van no vuelven nunca,
todo el mundo lo sabe,
y entre el claro gentío de los vientos
es inútil quejarse.
¿Verdad, chopo, maestro de la brisa?
¡Es inútil quejarse!

  Sin ningún viento,
  ¡hazme caso!
  Gira, corazón;
  gira, corazón.

Los encuentros de un caracol aventurero

Diciembre de 1918

(Granada)

A Ramón P. Roda

  Hay dulzura infantil
en la mañana quieta.
Los árboles extienden

My soul-armoire is overgrown with moss
and I've lost the key.

Without any wind,
pay heed to me!
Spin around, my heart;
spin around, my heart.

Breezes, gnomes, and winds
from nowhere,
gnats of the rose
with petals like pyramids,
trade winds weaned
among the rough trees,
flutes in the storm,
leave me!
My memory
has sturdy chains,
and captive is that bird
which sketches the afternoon
with its warbling.

The things that depart never return,
as everyone knows,
and amid the bright throng of the winds
it's pointless to lament.
Isn't that so, black-poplar, teacher of the breeze?
It's pointless to lament!

Without any wind,
pay heed to me!
Spin around, my heart;
spin around, my heart.

The Encounters of a Venturesome Snail

December 1918

(Granada)

To Ramón P. Roda

There is childlike sweetness
in the still morning.
The trees lower

sus brazos a la tierra.
Un vaho tembloroso
cubre las sementeras,
y las arañas tienden
sus caminos de seda
—rayas al cristal limpio
del aire—.
      En la alameda
un manantial recita
su canto entre las hierbas.
Y el caracol, pacífico
burgués de la vereda,
ignorado y humilde,
el paisaje contempla.
La divina quietud
de la Naturaleza
le dio valor y fe,
y olvidando las penas
de su hogar, deseó
ver el fin de la senda.

Echó a andar e internóse
en un bosque de yedras
y de ortigas. En medio
había dos ranas viejas
que tomaban el sol,
aburridas y enfermas.

«Estos cantos modernos
—murmuraba una de ellas—
son inútiles.» «Todos,
amiga —le contesta
la otra rana, que estaba
herida y casi ciega—.
Cuando joven creía
que si al fin Dios oyera
nuestro canto, tendría
compasión. Y mi ciencia,
pues ya he vivido mucho,
hace que no lo crea.
Yo ya no canto más . . .»

      Las dos ranas se quejan

their arms to the ground.
A wavering vapor
covers the sown fields,
and the spiders stretch out
their silken paths—
lines across the clean crystal
of the air.
          In the poplar grove
a spring recites
its song amid the grass.
And the snail, peaceful
citizen of the trail,
unknown and humble,
contemplates the landscape.
The divine stillness
of Nature
has lent him courage and faith,
and, forgetting the sorrows
of his home, he has conceived a desire
to see the end of the path.

    He started walking and he entered
a forest of ivy
and nettles. Midway
there were two old frogs
basking in the sun,
bored, ailing old ladies.

    "These modern songs,"
one of them muttered,
"are meaningless." "They all are,
my friend," replied
the other frog, who was
injured and nearly blind;
"when I was young I thought
that if God finally heard
our singing, he'd show
compassion. But the knowledge I've acquired,
for I have lived a long time,
causes me to disbelieve it.
Now I don't sing any more." . . .

    The two frogs complain,

pidiendo una limosna
a una ranita nueva
que pasa presumida
apartando las hierbas.
Ante el bosque sombrío
el caracol, se aterra.
Quiere gritar. No puede.
Las ranas se le acercan.

«¿Es una mariposa?»,
dice la casi ciega.
«Tiene dos cuernecitos
—la otra rana contesta—.
Es el caracol. ¿Vienes,
caracol, de otras tierras?»

«Vengo de mi casa y quiero
volverme muy pronto a ella.»
«Es un bicho muy cobarde
—exclama la rana ciega—.
¿No cantas nunca?» «No canto»,
dice el caracol. «¿Ni rezas?»
«Tampoco: nunca aprendí.»
«¿Ni crees en la vida eterna?»
«¿Qué es eso?»
          «Pues vivir siempre
en el agua más serena,
junto a una tierra florida
que a un rico manjar sustenta.»

«Cuando niño a mí me dijo
un día mi pobre abuela
que al morirme yo me iría
sobre las hojas más tiernas
de los árboles más altos.»

«Una hereje era tu abuela.
La verdad te la decimos
nosotras. Creerás en ella»,
dicen las ranas furiosas.

«¿Por qué quise ver la senda?
—gime el caracol—. Sí, creo

begging for alms
from a young little frog
who passes by, conceitedly,
shoving apart the blades of grass.

Faced with the dark forest,
the snail becomes frightened.
He tries to cry out. He can't.
The frogs approach him.

"Is it a butterfly?"
the nearly blind one asks.
"He's got two little horns,"
the other frog replies;
"it's the snail. Snail,
are you arriving from other lands?"

"I'm coming from my home, and I want
to return there as soon as I can."
"He's a very cowardly creature!"
the blind frog exclaims.
"Don't you ever sing?" "I don't sing,"
says the snail. "Or pray, either?"
"No: I never learned how."
"Don't you believe in life eternal?"
"What is it?"
                    "Why, living always
in the calmest water,
next to a blossoming soil
which produces plenty to eat."

"When I was a boy, I was told
one day by my late grandmother
that when I died I'd depart
above the tenderest leaves
of the tallest trees."

"Your grandmother was a heretic.
The truth is what you're hearing
from us. Believe it,"
the enraged frogs say.

"Why did I want to see the path?"
moans the snail. "Yes, I believe

por siempre en la vida eterna
que predicáis . . .»
          Las ranas,
muy pensativas, se alejan,
y el caracol, asustado,
se va perdiendo en la selva.

Las dos ranas mendigas
como esfinges se quedan.
Una de ellas pregunta:
«¿Crees tú en la vida eterna?»
«Yo no», dice muy triste
la rana herida y ciega.
«¿Por qué hemos dicho entonces
al caracol que crea?»
«¿Por qué? . . . No sé por qué
–dice la rana ciega–.
Me lleno de emoción
al sentir la firmeza
con que llaman mis hijos
a Dios desde la acequia . . .»
          El pobre caracol
vuelve atrás. Ya en la senda
un silencio ondulado
mana de la alameda.
Con un grupo de hormigas
encarnadas se encuentra.
Van muy alborotadas,
arrastrando tras ellas
a otra hormiga que tiene
tronchadas las antenas.
El caracol exclama:
«Hormiguitas, paciencia.
¿Por qué así maltratáis
a vuestra compañera?
Contadme lo que ha hecho.
Yo juzgaré en conciencia.
Cuéntalo tú, hormiguita.»

          La hormiga medio muerta
dice muy tristemente:
«Yo he visto las estrellas.»

forever in the life eternal
that you preach." . . .
                    The frogs
move off very pensively,
and the frightened snail
loses his way more and more in the woods.

    The two beggar frogs
remain like sphinxes.
One of them asks:
"Do you believe in life eternal?"
"Not me," is the very sad reply
of the injured, blind frog.
"Then, why did we tell
the snail to believe?"
"Why? . . . I don't know why,"
says the blind frog.
"I get filled with emotion
when I hear how staunchly
my children call
to God from the irrigation ditch." . . .

    The poor snail
turns back. By now on the path
waves of silence
emanate from the poplar grove.
He encounters a group
of red ants.
They are in a great commotion,
dragging after them
another ant who has
her antennae snapped.
The snail exclaims:
"Little ants, be patient!
Why do you so mistreat
your companion?
Tell me what she did.
I'll be a conscientious judge.
You, little ant, tell me."

    The half-dead ant
says very sadly:
"I saw the stars."

«¿Qué son estrellas?», dicen
las hormigas inquietas.
Y el caracol pregunta
pensativo: «¿Estrellas?»
«Sí –repite la hormiga–.
He visto las estrellas.
Subí al árbol más alto
que tiene la alameda
y vi miles de ojos
dentro de mis tinieblas.»
El caracol pregunta:
«¿Pero qué son estrellas?»
«Son luces que llevamos
sobre nuestra cabeza.»
«Nosotras no las vemos»,
las hormigas comentan.
Y el caracol: «Mi vista
sólo alcanza a las hierbas.»

Las hormigas exclaman
moviendo sus antenas:
«Te mataremos, eres
perezosa y perversa.
El trabajo es tu ley.»

«Yo he visto a las estrellas»,
dice la hormiga herida.
Y el caracol sentencia:
«Dejadla que se vaya,
seguid vuestras faenas.
Es fácil que muy pronto
ya rendida se muera.»

Por el aire dulzón
ha cruzado una abeja.
La hormiga, agonizando,
huele la tarde inmensa
y dice: «Es la que viene
a llevarme a una estrella.»

Las demás hormiguitas
huyen al verla muerta.

El caracol suspira

"What are stars?" say
the nervous ants.
And the snail asks
pensively: "Stars?"
"Yes," the ant repeats;
"I saw the stars.
I climbed the tallest tree
in the poplar grove
and I saw thousands of eyes
within my darkness."
The snail asks:
"But what are stars?"
"They're lights we wear
over our head."
"We don't see them,"
is the comment of the ants.
And the snail: "My eyes
see only as far as the grass."

The ants exclaim,
waving their antennae:
"We'll kill you, ant, you're
lazy and perverse.
The law for you is: labor!"

"I saw the stars,"
the wounded ant says.
And the snail's sentence is:
"Let her depart;
the rest of you continue your tasks.
Most likely she'll die
very soon of her exhaustion."

In the sickly-sweet air
a bee crosses by.
The ant, in her death throes,
smells the gigantic afternoon
and says: "She's the one coming
to take me to a star."

All the other ants
flee when they see her dead.

The snail sighs

y aturdido se aleja
lleno de confusión
por lo eterno. «La senda
no tiene fin –exclama–.
Acaso a las estrellas
se llegue por aquí.
Pero mi gran torpeza
me impedirá llegar.
No hay que pensar en ellas.»
Todo estaba brumoso
de sol débil y niebla.
Campanarios lejanos
llaman gente a la iglesia,
y el caracol, pacífico
burgués de la vereda,
aturdido e inquieto
el paisaje contempla.

Canción primaveral

28 de marzo de 1919

(Granada)

I

Salen los niños alegres
de la escuela,
poniendo en el aire tibio
del Abril, canciones tiernas.
¡Qué alegría tiene el hondo
silencio de la calleja!
Un silencio hecho pedazos
por risas de plata nueva.

II

Voy camino de la tarde
entre flores de la huerta
dejando sobre el camino
el agua de mi tristeza.
En el monte solitario
un cementerio de aldea

and, his mind numb, departs,
filled with confusion
about eternity. "The path
has no end!" he exclaims;
"maybe it's in this direction
that one reaches the stars.
But my great clumsiness
will keep me from getting there.
I mustn't think about them."

Everything was foggy
from weak sunshine and mist.
Distant steeple bells
are summoning people to church,
and the snail, peaceful
citizen of the trail,
dumbfounded and restless,
contemplates the landscape.

Spring Song

March 28, 1919

(Granada)

I

The joyous children leave
the school,
sending gentle songs
into the warm April air.
What joy there is in the deep
silence of the lane!
A silence shattered
by laughter like new silver.

II

I'm on my way to the evening,
walking amid the flowers of the fertile plain
and leaving behind on the path
the waters of my sadness.
On the lonely hill
a village cemetery

parece un campo sembrado
con granos de calaveras.
Y han florecido cipreses
como gigantes cabezas
que con órbitas vacías
y verdosas cabelleras
pensativos y dolientes
el horizonte contemplan.

¡Abril divino, que vienes
cargado de sol y esencias,
llena con nidos de oro
las floridas calaveras!

Canción menor

Diciembre de 1918
(Granada)

Tienen gotas de rocío
las alas del ruiseñor,
gotas claras de la luna
cuajadas por su ilusión.

Tiene el mármol de la fuente
el beso del surtidor,
sueño de estrellas humildes.

Las niñas de los jardines
me dicen todas adiós
cuando paso. Las campanas
también me dicen adiós.
Y los árboles se besan
en el crepúsculo. Yo
voy llorando por la calle,
grotesco y sin solución,
con tristeza de Cyrano
y de Quijote,
                    redentor
de imposibles infinitos

is like a field sown
with skulls for seeds.
And cypresses have blossomed
like gigantic heads
which, with empty eye-sockets
and greenish hair,
pensively and sorrowfully
scan the horizon.

Divine April, you that come
laden with sunshine and perfumes,
fill with golden nests
the blossoming skulls!

Minor Song

December 1918

(Granada)

There are dewdrops
on the nightingale's wings,
bright drops of moonlight
formed by his high hopes.

The marble of the fountain has
the kiss of its jet,
a dream of humble stars.[1]

The girls in the gardens
all say good-bye to me
as I pass. The church bells
also say good-bye to me.
And the trees kiss one another
in the dusk. I
go down the street weeping,
grotesque and unresolved,
as sad as Cyrano
and Quixote,[2]
                a redeemer
of impossible infinities

---

1. Some editors deduce from the structure of the poem that a line has dropped out here, a line assonating in *o*.   2. Two dreamers unlucky in love.

con el ritmo del reloj.
Y veo secarse los lirios
al contacto de mi voz
manchada de luz sangrienta,
y en mi lírica canción
llevo galas de payaso
empolvado. El amor
bello y lindo se ha escondido
bajo una araña. El sol
como otra araña me oculta
con sus patas de oro. No
conseguiré mi ventura,
pues soy como el mismo Amor,
cuyas flechas son de llanto,
y el carcaj el corazón

    Daré todo a los demás
y lloraré mi pasión
como niño abandonado
en cuento que se borró.

Elegía a Doña Juana la Loca

Diciembre de 1918
(Granada)

A Melchor Fernández Almagro

    Princesa enamorada sin ser correspondida.
Clavel rojo en un valle profundo y desolado.
La tumba que te guarda rezuma tu tristeza
a través de los ojos que ha abierto sobre el mármol.

    Eras una paloma con alma gigantesca
cuyo nido fue sangre del suelo castellano.
Derramaste tu fuego sobre un cáliz de nieve
y al querer alentarlo tus alas se troncharon.

    Soñabas que tu amor fuera como el infante
que te sigue sumiso recogiendo tu manto.
Y en vez de flores, versos y collares de perlas
te dio la Muerte rosas marchitas en un ramo.

to the rhythm of my watch.
And I see the irises dry up
at the sound of my voice,
which is stained with bloody light,
and in my lyric song
I wear the finery of a powdered
clown. Love,
handsome and charming, has hidden
under a spider. The sun,
like another spider, conceals me
with its golden legs. I shall not
accomplish my good fortune,
because I am like Love himself,
whose arrows are of tears,
whose quiver is the heart.

I shall give away everything to others,
and I shall beweep my passion
like a forsaken child
in a half-forgotten fairy tale.

Elegy to Queen Juana the Mad

December 1918

(Granada)

To Melchor Fernández Almagro

Princess whose love was unrequited.
Red carnation in a deep, desolate valley.
The tomb that protects you exudes your sadness
through the eyeholes it has opened in its marble.

You were a dove with a gigantic soul
whose nest was blood of the Castilian soil.
You poured your fire onto a chalice of snow
and in your attempt to fan the flame your wings broke.

You dreamed that your love might be like the child
who follows you submissively, gathering up your mantle.
But instead of flowers, poetry, and pearl necklaces
Death gave you faded roses on a sprig.

Tenías en el pecho la formidable aurora
de Isabel de Segura, Melibea. Tu canto,
como alondra que mira quebrarse el horizonte,
se torna de repente monótono y amargo.

Y tu grito estremece los cimientos de Burgos.
Y oprime la salmodia del coro cartujano.
Y choca con los ecos de las lentas campanas
perdiéndose en la sombra tembloroso y rasgado.

Tenías la pasión que da el cielo de España.
La pasión del puñal, de la ojera y el llanto.
¡Oh princesa divina de crepúsculo rojo,
con la rueca de hierro y de acero lo hilado!
Nunca tuviste el nido, ni el madrigal doliente,
ni el laúd juglaresco que solloza lejano.
Tu juglar fue un mancebo con escamas de plata
y un eco de trompeta su acento enamorado.

Y, sin embargo, estabas para el amor formada,
hecha para el suspiro, el mimo y el desmayo.
Para llorar tristeza sobre el pecho querido
deshojando una rosa de olor entre los labios.

Para mirar la luna bordada sobre el río
y sentir la nostalgia que en sí lleva el rebaño.
Y mirar los eternos jardines de la sombra.
¡Oh princesa morena que duermes bajo el mármol!

¿Tienes los ojos negros abiertos a la luz?
O se enredan serpientes a tus senos exhaustos . . .
¿Dónde fueron tus besos lanzados a los vientos?
¿Dónde fue la tristeza de tu amor desgraciado?
En el cofre de plomo, dentro de tu esqueleto,
tendrás el corazón partido en mil pedazos.

Y Granada te guarda como santa reliquia,
¡oh princesa morena que duermes bajo el mármol!
Eloísa y Julieta fueron dos margaritas

In your bosom you had the formidable dawn
of Isabel de Segura, Melibea.[3] Your song,
like a lark watching the horizon break open,
suddenly becomes monotonous and bitter.

And your cry shakes the foundations of Burgos.
And it drowns out the psalmody of the Carthusian choir.
And it clashes with the echoes of the slow church bells
dying away in the trembling, torn darkness.

You possessed the passion which the sky of Spain gives.
The passion of the dagger, of ringed eyes, and of weeping.
O divine princess of red twilight,
with a distaff of iron and spun thread of steel!
You never had a nest, or a sorrowful madrigal,
or a minstrel's lute sobbing in the distance.
Your minstrel was a lad with silver scales of armor,
whose loving tones were the echo of a battle trumpet.

And yet, you were fashioned for love,
made for sighs, caresses, and swoons.
Made to weep out your sadness on a beloved breast,
stripping a fragrant rose of its petals between your lips.

Made to gaze at the moonlight embroidered on the river
and to feel the nostalgia that flocks bring with them.
And to gaze at the eternal gardens of darkness.
O swarthy princess asleep beneath the marble!

Are your dark eyes open to the light?
Or do serpents entwine your drained breasts? . . .
What became of the kisses you flung to the winds?
What became of the grief of your unfortunate love?
In the lead coffin, inside your skeleton,
your heart must be broken into a thousand pieces.

And Granada keeps you like a holy relic,
O swarthy princess asleep beneath the marble!
Héloïse and Juliet were two daisies

---

3. Isabel is one of the legendary star-crossed "lovers of Teruel [in Aragon]" who sup-
posedly lived in the 13th century. Melibea, heroine of the great play *La Celestina* (by
Fernando de Rojas, ca. 1500), dies of love. With punctuation as in the text, Melibea
can be taken as a vocative, equating her with Juana; or possibly the translation could
be "of Isabel de Segura, of Melibea." In some editions the comma after "Segura" is a
period.

pero tú fuiste un rojo clavel ensangrentado,
que vino de la tierra dorada de Castilla
a dormir entre nieves y cipresales castos.

Granada era tu lecho de muerte, Doña Juana;
los cipreses tus cirios;
la sierra tu retablo.
Un retablo de nieve que mitigue tus ansias
¡con el agua que pasa junto a ti! ¡La del Dauro!

Granada era tu lecho de muerte, Doña Juana,
la de las torres viejas y del jardín callado,
la de la yedra muerta sobre los muros rojos,
la de la niebla azul y el arrayán romántico.

Princesa enamorada y mal correspondida.
Clavel rojo en un valle profundo y desolado.
La tumba que te guarda rezuma tu tristeza
a través de los ojos que ha abierto sobre el mármol.

¡Cigarra!

3 de agosto de 1918
(Fuente Vaqueros, Granada)

A María Luisa

¡Cigarra!
¡Dichosa tú!
Que sobre lecho de tierra
mueres borracha de luz.

Tú sabes de las campiñas
el secreto de la vida,
y el cuento del hada vieja
que nacer hierba sentía
en ti quedóse guardado.

¡Cigarra!
¡Dichosa tú!
Pues mueres bajo la sangre
de un corazón todo azul.

but you were a blood-red carnation
that came from the gilded land of Castile
to sleep amid snows and chaste cypress groves.

Granada was your deathbed, Queen Juana;
the cypresses, your tapers;
the sierra your altarpiece.
A snowy altarpiece to alleviate your anxiety
with the water that flows beside you! That of the Dauro!

Granada was your deathbed, Queen Juana,
city of ancient towers and quiet gardens,
city of dead ivy on red walls,
city of blue mist and romantic myrtle.

Princess in love but unrequited.
Red carnation in a deep, desolate valley.
The tomb that protects you exudes your sadness
through the eyes it has opened in its marble.

Cicada!

August 3, 1918

(Fuente Vaqueros, Granada)

To María Luisa

Cicada!
How lucky you are!
For on a bed of earth
you die drunken with light.

You have learned from the countryside
the secret of life,
and the tale of the ancient fairy
who could hear the grass grow
is preserved in your memory.

Cicada!
How lucky you are!
For you die beneath the blood
of a heart that is all blue.

La luz es Dios que desciende,
y el sol,
brecha por donde se filtra.
¡Cigarra!
¡Dichosa tú!
Pues sientes en la agonía
todo el peso del azul.

Todo lo vivo que pasa
por las puertas de la muerte
va con la cabeza baja
y un aire blanco durmiente.
Con habla de pensamiento.
Sin sonidos . . .
Tristemente,
cubierto con el silencio
que es el manto de la muerte.

Mas tú, cigarra encantada,
derramando son te mueres
y quedas trasfigurada
en sonido y luz celeste.
¡Cigarra!
¡Dichosa tú!
Pues te envuelve con su manto
el propio Espíritu Santo,
que es la luz.

¡Cigarra!
Estrella sonora
sobre los campos dormidos,
vieja amiga de las ranas
y de los oscuros grillos,
tienes sepulcros de oro
en los rayos tremolinos
del sol que dulce te hiere
en la fuerza del Estío,
y el sol se lleva tu alma
para hacerla luz.

Sea mi corazón cigarra
sobre los campos divinos.
Que muera cantando lento

The light is God descending;
and the sun,
the breach through which it filters.

Cicada!
How lucky you are!
For when you die you feel
the full weight of the blue.

All living things that pass
through the portals of death
walk with head bowed
and the white air of a sleeper.
Their speech is thought.
Soundless . . .
Sadly,
covered with the silence
that is the mantle of death.

But you, enchanted cicada,
you die pouring forth music
and you become transfigured
into sound and celestial light.

Cicada!
How lucky you are!
For the Holy Spirit itself,
which is light,
wraps you in its mantle.

Cicada!
Resounding star
above the sleeping fields,
old friend of the frogs
and of the obscure crickets,
you have golden sepulchers
in the quivering rays
of the sun that strikes you gently
in the strength of Summer,
and the sun carries off your soul
to make it shining light.

May my heart be a cicada
on the divine fields!
May it die with a slow song

por el cielo azul herido
y cuando esté ya expirando
una mujer que adivino
lo derrame con sus manos
por el polvo.

Y mi sangre sobre el campo
sea rosado y dulce limo
donde claven sus azadas
los cansados campesinos.

¡Cigarra!
¡Dichosa tú!
Pues te hieren las espadas invisibles
del azul.

Balada triste

Pequeño poema

Abril de 1918
(Granada)

¡Mi corazón es una mariposa,
niños buenos del prado!,
que presa por la araña gris del tiempo
tiene el polen fatal del desengaño.

De niño yo canté como vosotros,
niños buenos del prado,
solté mi gavilán con las temibles
cuatro uñas de gato.
Pasé por el jardín de Cartagena,
la verbena invocando,
y perdí la sortija de mi dicha
al pasar el arroyo imaginario.

Fui también caballero
una tarde fresquita de mayo.
Ella era entonces para mí el enigma,
estrella azul sobre mi pecho intacto.

in the wounded blue sky,
and when it is on the point of death
may a woman, one whom I guess,
pour it out with her hands
onto the dust!

   And may my blood on the field
be moist soil, pink and soft,
into which the weary farmers
can thrust their hoes.

   Cicada!
How lucky you are!
For you are wounded by the invisible swords
of the blue.

Sad Ballad

Small Poem

April 1918

(Granada)

   My heart is a butterfly,
good children of the meadow,
which, captured by the gray spider of time,
possesses the fatal pollen of disillusionment!

   As a boy I sang just like you,
good children of the meadow,
I loosed my sparrow hawk with its dread
four catlike talons.
I passed through the garden of Cartagena,
invoking the vervain,
and I lost my lucky ring
when crossing the imaginary stream.[4]

   I was also a knight
on one cool May afternoon.
At that time "she" was a riddle to me,
a blue star on my untouched breast.

---

4. This sentence recalls several nursery rhymes and play songs, especially one about losing a ring while crossing the "stream of Santa Clara."

Cabalgué lentamente hacia los cielos,
era un domingo de pipirigallo,
y vi que en vez de rosas y claveles
ella tronchaba lirios con sus manos.

Yo siempre fui intranquilo,
niños buenos del prado,
el *ella* del romance me sumía
en ensoñares claros.
¿Quién será la que coge los claveles
y las rosas de mayo?
¿Y por qué la verán sólo los niños
a lomos de Pegaso?
¿Será esa misma la que en los rondones
con tristeza llamamos
Estrella, suplicándole que salga
a danzar por el campo? . . .

En abril de mi infancia yo cantaba,
niños buenos del prado,
la *ella* impenetrable del romance
donde sale Pegaso.
Yo decía en las noches la tristeza
de mi amor ignorado,
y la luna lunera, ¡qué sonrisa
ponía entre sus labios!
¿Quién será la que corta los claveles
y las rosas de mayo?
Y de aquella chiquita, tan bonita,
que su madre ha casado,
¿en qué oculto rincón de cementerio
dormirá su fracaso?

Yo solo con mi amor desconocido,
sin corazón, sin llantos,
hacia el techo imposible de los cielos
con un gran sol por báculo.

¡Qué tristeza tan seria me da sombra!,
niños buenos del prado,
cómo recuerda dulce el corazón
los días ya lejanos . . .
¿Quién será la que corta las claveles
y las rosas de mayo?

I slowly rode my steed into the skies
on that Sunday of sainfoin,
and I saw that, in place of roses and carnations,
she was snapping irises with her hands.

   I was always restless,
good children of the meadow,
the "she" of old ballads immersed me
in bright daydreams.
Who will be the woman picking the carnations
and the roses of May?
And why will she be seen only by the children
who are astride Pegasus?
Will she be the same woman whom in our round games
we sadly call
Star, imploring her to come out
and dance in the field? . . .

   In the April of my childhood I would sing,
good children of the meadow,
about the unfathomable "she" of the ballad
in which Pegasus appears.
At night I'd recite the sorrow
of my neglected love,
and the moon-moon, what a smile
it placed on her lips!
Who will be the woman cutting the carnations
and the roses of May?
And that young girl, so pretty,
whom her mother married off,
in what hidden corner of a cemetery
can her failed life be sleeping?

   I alone with my unrecognized love,
without a heart, without tears,
heading for the impossible ceiling of the skies
with a big sun for a staff.

   What a serious sorrow shades me,
good children of the meadow,
how my heart tenderly recalls
those already distant days! . . .
Who will be the woman cutting the carnations
and the roses of May?

La sombra de mi alma

Diciembre de 1919
(Madrid)

La sombra de mi alma
huye por un ocaso de alfabetos,
niebla de libros
y palabras.
¡La sombra de mi alma!

He llegado a la línea donde cesa
la nostalgia,
y la gota de llanto se transforma
alabastro de espíritu.
(¡La sombra de mi alma!)

El copo del dolor
se acaba,
pero queda la razón y la sustancia
de mi viejo mediodía de labios,
de mi viejo mediodía
de miradas.

Un turbio laberinto
de estrellas ahumadas
enreda mi ilusión
casi marchita.
¡La sombra de mi alma!

Y una alucinación
me ordeña las miradas.
Veo la palabra amor
desmoronada.

¡Ruiseñor mío!
¡Ruiseñor!
¿Aún cantas?

The Shadow of My Soul

December 1919
(Madrid)

The shadow of my soul
flees through a sunset of alphabets,
a mist of books
and words.

The shadow of my soul!

I have reached the line where
nostalgia ceases,
and the teardrop is transformed
into spiritual alabaster.[5]

The shadow of my soul!

The balled yarn of my grief
is running out,
but reason remains, as does the substance
of my old noonday of lips,
of my old noonday
of glances.

A confused labyrinth
of smoky stars
entangles my hopes,
which are nearly faded.

The shadow of my soul!

And a hallucination
milks my gaze.
I see the word "love"
crumbled to bits.

My nightingale!
Nightingale!
Are you still singing?

---

5. Or: "the teardrop, spiritual alabaster, is transformed." Some editors add a comma after *transforma*.

Lluvia

Enero de 1919

(Granada)

La lluvia tiene un vago secreto de ternura,
algo de soñolencia resignada y amable.
Una música humilde se despierta con ella
que hace vibrar el alma dormida del paisaje.

Es un besar azul que recibe la Tierra,
el mito primitivo que vuelve a realizarse.
El contacto ya frío de cielo y tierra viejos
con una mansedumbre de atardecer constante.

Es la aurora del fruto. La que nos trae las flores
y nos unge de espíritu santo de los mares.
La que derrama vida sobre las sementeras
y en el alma tristeza de lo que no se sabe.

La nostalgia terrible de una vida perdida,
el fatal sentimiento de haber nacido tarde,
o la ilusión inquieta de un mañana imposible
con la inquietud cercana del dolor de la carne.

El amor se despierta en el gris de su ritmo,
nuestro cielo interior tiene un triunfo de sangre,
pero nuestro optimismo se convierte en tristeza
al contemplar las gotas muertas en los cristales.

Y son las gotas: ojos de infinito que miran
al infinito blanco que les sirvió de madre.

Cada gota de lluvia tiembla en el cristal turbio
y le dejan divinas heridas de diamante.
Son poetas del agua que han visto y que meditan
lo que la muchedumbre de los ríos no sabe.

¡Oh lluvia silenciosa sin tormentas ni vientos,
lluvia mansa y serena de esquila y luz suave,
lluvia buena y pacífica que eres la verdadera,
la que amorosa y triste sobre las cosas caes!

¡Oh lluvia franciscana que llevas a tus gotas
almas de fuentes claras y humildes manantiales!

Rain

January 1919
(Granada)

The rain has a vague secret of tenderness,
something resignedly and amiably somnolent.
With it there awakes a humble music
that makes the sleeping soul of the landscape vibrate.

It is a blue kiss that the Earth receives,
the primal myth that once again comes true.
The already cold contact of the old sky and earth
with a gentleness like that of a perpetual coming of evening.

It is the dawn of the fruit. The dawn brought to us by the flowers,
anointing us with the holy spirit of the seas.
The dawn that sheds life upon the sown fields
and, in our soul, the sadness of the unknown.

The dreadful nostalgia for a wasted life,
the fatal feeling that you were born too late,
or the restless hope for an impossible morning
with the nearby restlessness of the flesh's ache.

Love awakens in the gray of its rhythm,
our inner sky enjoys a triumph of blood,
but our optimism is changed to sadness
when we observe the dead drops on the panes.

And the drops are eyes of infinity which gaze
at the white infinity which served them as mother.

Each raindrop trembles on the clouded glass,
leaving behind on it divine diamond-scratches.
They are watery poets who have seen, and meditate on,
that which the multitude of rivers doesn't know.

O silent rain without tempests or winds,
gentle, calm rain, like sheep bells and soft light,
good, peaceful rain—the real kind—
which falls on every object lovingly and sadly!

O Franciscan rain, carrying in your drops
the souls of bright fountains and humble springs!

Cuando sobre los campos desciendes lentamente
las rosas de mi pecho con tus sonidos abres.

El canto primitivo que dices al silencio
y la historia sonora que cuentas al ramaje
los comenta llorando mi corazón desierto
en un negro y profundo pentágrama sin clave.

Mi alma tiene tristeza de la lluvia serena,
tristeza resignada de cosa irrealizable,
tengo en el horizonte un lucero encendido
y el corazón me impide que corra a contemplarle.

¡Oh lluvia silenciosa que los árboles aman
y eres sobre el piano dulzura emocionante,
das al alma las mismas nieblas y resonancias
que pones en el alma dormida del paisaje!

Elegía

Diciembre de 1918

(Granada)

Como un incensario lleno de deseos,
pasas en la tarde luminosa y clara
con la carne oscura de nardo marchito
y el sexo potente sobre tu mirada.

Llevas en la boca tu melancolía
de pureza muerta, y en la dionisiaca
copa de tu vientre la araña que teje
el velo infecundo que cubre la entraña
nunca florecida con las vivas rosas,
fruto de los besos.

En tus manos blancas
llevas la madeja de tus ilusiones,
muertas para siempre, y sobre tu alma
la pasión hambrienta de besos de fuego
y tu amor de madre que sueña lejanas
visiones de cunas en ambientes quietos,
hilando en los labios lo azul de la nana.

When you descend slowly onto the fields
you open the roses of my breast with your sounds.

The primal song you sing to the silence
and the sonorous story you narrate to the boughs
are commented on tearfully by my barren heart
in a black, deep stave of music without a key.

My soul has the sadness of the calm rain,
a resigned sadness for something unattainable;
on my horizon I have a blazing star
but my heart keeps me from running to gaze at it.

O silent rain which the trees love,
you that are sweet excitement on the piano,
you lend my soul the same mists and resonances
which you give to the sleeping soul of the landscape!

Elegy

December 1918

(Granada)

Like a censer filled with desires,
you go by in the luminous, bright afternoon
with your dark skin like a faded amaryllis
and your sex potent in your gaze.

You wear on your lips your melancholy
born of dead purity; and, in the Dionysiac
goblet of your belly, the spider that weaves
the infertile web covering the womb
which has never blossomed with living roses,
fruit of kisses.

In your white hands
you bear the skein of your hopes,
dead forever, and in your soul
the hungry passion for fiery kisses
and your maternal love, dreaming distant
visions of cradles in quiet surroundings,
as you spin on your lips the blue thread of lullabies.

Como Ceres dieras tus espigas de oro
si el amor dormido tu cuerpo tocara,
y como la virgen María pudieras
brotar de tus senos otra Vía Láctea.

Te marchitarás como la magnolia.
Nadie besará tus muslos de brasa.
Ni a tu cabellera llegarán los dedos
que la pulsen como
                    las cuerdas de un arpa.

¡Oh mujer potente de ébano y de nardo!,
cuyo aliento tiene blancor de biznagas.
Venus del mantón de Manila que sabe
del vino de Málaga y de la guitarra.

¡Oh cisne moreno!, cuyo lago tiene
lotos de saetas, olas de naranjas
y espumas de rojos claveles que aroman
los nidos marchitos que hay bajo sus alas.

Nadie te fecunda. Mártir andaluza,
tus besos debieron ser bajo una parra
plenos del silencio que tiene la noche
y del ritmo turbio del agua estancada.

Pero tus ojeras se van agrandando
y tu pelo negro va siendo de plata;
tus senos resbalan escanciando aromas
y empieza a curvarse tu espléndida espalda.

¡Oh mujer esbelta, maternal y ardiente!
Virgen dolorosa que tiene clavadas
todas las estrellas del cielo profundo
en su corazón, ya sin esperanza.

Eres el espejo de una Andalucía
que sufre pasiones gigantes y calla,
pasiones mecidas por los abanicos
y por las mantillas sobre las gargantas
que tienen temblores de sangre, de nieve
y arañazos rojos hechos por miradas.

Te vas por la niebla del Otoño, virgen
como Inés, Cecilia y la dulce Clara,

Like Ceres, you would have given away your golden grain
if sleeping love had touched your body,
and like the Virgin Mary you would have been able
to make another Milky Way well up from your breasts.

You will fade like the magnolia.
No one will kiss your red-hot thighs.
Nor will there come to your hair the fingers
that might strum it like
                    the strings of a harp.

O woman potent with ebony and spikenard,
whose breath has the whiteness of jasmine!
A Venus in a Manila shawl, with the savor of
Málaga wine and guitars.

O dark swan, whose lake contains
lotuses of devotional hymns, waves of oranges,
and the froth of red carnations which perfume
the withered nests it has under its wings!

No one makes you fertile. Andalusian martyr,
your kisses beneath a grapevine should have been
full of the silence which the night possesses
and of the murky rhythm of dammed-up waters.

But the rings around your eyes are growing wider
and your black hair is turning silver;
your breasts trickle, pouring fragrance like cupbearers,
and your magnificent shoulders are beginning to droop.

O slender, maternal, ardent woman!
Sorrowful Virgin with all the stars
of the lofty sky planted
in her heart, without hope by this time.

You are the mirror of an Andalusia
that suffers gigantic passions and remains silent,
passions rocked to sleep by fans
and by mantillas covering throats
that have tremors of blood, of snow,
and red scratches made by staring eyes.

You depart in the mist of Autumn, as virginal
as Saints Agnes, Cecilia, and sweet Clare,

siendo una bacante que hubiera danzado
de pámpanos verdes y vid coronada.

La tristeza inmensa que flota en tus ojos
nos dice tu vida rota y fracasada,
la monotonía de tu ambiente pobre
viendo pasar gente desde tu ventana,
oyendo la lluvia sobre la amargura
que tiene la vieja calle provinciana,
mientras que a lo lejos suenan los clamores
turbios y confusos de unas campanadas.

Mas en vano escuchaste los acentos del aire.
Nunca llegó a tu oído la dulce serenata.
Detrás de tus cristales aún miras anhelante.
¡Qué tristeza tan honda tendrás dentro del alma
al sentir en el pecho ya cansado y exhausto
la pasión de una niña recién enamorada!

Tu cuerpo irá a la tumba
intacto de emociones.
Sobre la oscura tierra
brotará una alborada.
De tus ojos saldrán dos claveles sangrientos
y de tus senos rosas como la nieve blancas.
Pero tu gran tristeza se irá con las estrellas
como otra estrella digna de herirlas y eclipsarlas.

Santiago
Balada ingenua

25 de julio de 1918
(Fuente Vaqueros, Granada)

I

Esta noche ha pasado Santiago
su camino de luz en el cielo.
Lo comentan los niños jugando
con el agua de un cauce sereno.

¿Dónde va el peregrino celeste
por el claro infinito sendero?

though you're a bacchante who might have danced
wreathed with green tendrils and grapevines.

   The immense sadness swimming in your eyes
tells us of your broken, failed life,
the monotony of your poor surroundings
as you watch passersby from your window,
hearing the rain fall on the bitterness
which fills the old provincial street,
while in the distance resound the muffled,
confused clamors of church bells.

   But you listened in vain to the accents of the air.
A sweet serenade never reached your ears.
Behind your windows you still gaze yearningly.
What deep sorrow must lie within your soul
when you feel in your now exhausted and drained bosom
the passion of a girl who has just fallen in love!

   Your body will go to the grave
untouched by strong emotions.
From the dark earth
an aubade will well up.
From your eyes will sprout two blood-red carnations,
and, from your breasts, roses white as snow.
But your great sorrow will depart with the stars
like another star worthy of wounding and eclipsing them.

Saint James
Naïve Ballad
July 25, 1918
(Fuente Vaqueros, Granada)

I

   Tonight Saint James has traveled
his path of light in the sky.
The children discuss this as they play
with the waters of a calm channel.

   Where is the heavenly pilgrim going
across the bright, infinite trail?

Va a la aurora que brilla en el fondo
en caballo blanco como el hielo.

¡Niños chicos, cantad en el prado,
horadando con risas al viento!

Dice un hombre que ha visto a Santiago
en tropel con doscientos guerreros.
Iban todos cubiertos de luces,
con guirnaldas de verdes luceros,
y el caballo que monta Santiago
era un astro de brillos intensos.

Dice el hombre que cuenta la historia
que en la noche dormida se oyeron
tremolar plateado de alas
que en sus ondas llevóse el silencio.

¿Qué sería que el río paróse?
Eran ángeles los caballeros.

¡Niños chicos, cantad en el prado,
horadando con risas al viento!

Es la noche de luna menguante.
¡Escuchad! ¿Qué se siente en el cielo,
que los grillos refuerzan sus cuerdas
y dan voces los perros vegueros?

–Madre abuela, ¿cuál es el camino,
madre abuela, que yo no lo veo?

–Mira bien y verás una cinta
de polvillo harinoso y espeso,
un borrón que parece de plata
o de nácar. ¿Lo ves?
                    –Ya lo veo.

–Madre abuela, ¿dónde está Santiago?
–Por allí marcha con su cortejo,
la cabeza llena de plumajes
y de perlas muy finas el cuerpo,
con la luna rendida a sus plantas,
con el sol escondido en el pecho.

He is going to the dawn that shines in the background
on a horse white as ice.

　Little children, sing in the meadow,
making holes in the wind with your laughter!

　A man says he has seen Saint James
in a troupe of two hundred warriors.
They were all covered with gleaming armor,
garlanded with green evening-stars,
and the horse Saint James was riding
was a planet intensely bright.

　The man telling the story says[6]
that in the sleeping night was heard
a silvery trembling of wings
which the silence carried away on its waves.

　What could have made the river stop flowing?
The riders were angels.

　Little children, sing in the meadow,
making holes in the wind with your laughter!

　It's the night of the waning moon.
Listen! What is heard in the sky
that makes the crickets reinforce their strings
and the dogs in Granada's plain give voice?

　"Grandmother, which is the road,
grandmother? Because I don't see it."

　"Look hard and you'll see a ribbon
of thick, flourlike powder,
a blur resembling silver
or mother-of-pearl. See it?"
　　　　　　　　　　　"Now I do."

　"Grandmother, where is Saint James?"
"He's riding over there with his retinue,
his head bearing many plumes
and his body, very fine pearls,
with the moon submissive at his feet
and the sun hidden in his bosom."

---

6. Or, just possibly: "The man says that history relates."

Esta noche en la vega se escuchan
los relatos brumosos del cuento.

¡Niños chicos, cantad en el prado,
horadando con risas al viento!

II

Una vieja que vive muy pobre
en la parte más alta del pueblo,
que posee una rueca inservible,
una Virgen y dos gatos negros,
mientras hace la ruda calceta
con sus secos y temblones dedos,
rodeada de buenas comadres
y de sucios chiquillos traviesos,
en la paz de la noche tranquila,
con las sierras perdidas en negro,
va contando con ritmos tardíos
la visión que ella tuvo en sus tiempos.

Ella vio en una noche lejana
como ésta, sin ruidos ni vientos,
al apóstol Santiago en persona,
peregrino en la tierra del cielo.

—Y comadre, ¿cómo iba vestido?
—le preguntan dos voces a un tiempo—.

—Con bordón de esmeraldas y perlas
y una túnica de terciopelo.

Cuando hubo pasado la puerta,
mis palomas sus alas tendieron,
y mi perro, que estaba dormido,
fue tras él, sus pisadas lamiendo.
Era dulce el Apóstol divino,
más aún que la luna de Enero.
A su paso dejó por la senda
un olor de azucena y de incienso.

—Y comadre, ¿no le dijo nada?
—le preguntan dos voces a un tiempo—.

This night there are heard on the plain
the misty narratives of folktale.

Little children, sing in the meadow,
making holes in the wind with your laughter!

II

An old woman, living very humbly
in the highest part of the village,
owner of a now useless distaff,
an image of the Virgin, and two black cats,
while she does coarse knitting
with her dry, shaky fingers,
surrounded by good neighbor-women
and dirty, mischievous little children,
in the peace of the tranquil night,
with the mountain ranges lost in the blackness,
is relating at a slow pace
the vision she had in her younger days.

One night long ago, a night
like this one, without noise or wind, she saw
the apostle Saint James in person,
a pilgrim from the sky on earth.

"And, neighbor, how was he dressed?"
two voices ask at the same time.

"He had a pilgrim's staff of emeralds and pearls
and a velvet tunic."

After he passed my doorway,
my doves spread their wings,
and my dog, which had been sleeping,
followed him, licking his footprints.
The divine Apostle was gentle,
more so than the moon in January.
His paces down the path left behind them
a fragrance of lilies and incense.

"But, neighbor, did he say nothing to you?"
two voices ask at the same time.

–Al pasar me miró sonriente
y una estrella dejóme aquí dentro.
–¿Dónde tienes guardada esa estrella?
–le pregunta un chiquillo travieso–.
–¿Se ha apagado –dijéronle otros–
como cosa de un encantamiento?
–No, hijos míos, la estrella relumbra,
que en el alma clavada la llevo.
–¿Cómo son las estrellas aquí?
–Hijo mío, igual que en el cielo.
–Siga, siga la vieja comadre.
¿Dónde iba el glorioso viajero?
–Se perdió por aquellas montañas
con mis blancas palomas y el perro.
Pero llena dejóme la casa
de rosales y de jazmineros,
y las uvas verdes de la parra
maduraron, y mi troje lleno
encontré a la siguiente mañana.
Todo obra del Apóstol bueno.

–¡Grande suerte que tuvo, comadre!
–sermonean dos voces a un tiempo–.

Los chiquillos están ya dormidos
y los campos en hondo silencio.

¡Niños chicos, pensad en Santiago
por los turbios caminos del sueño!

¡Noche clara, finales de Julio!
¡Ha pasado Santiago en el cielo!
La tristeza que tiene mi alma,
por el blanco camino la dejo,
para ver si la encuentran los niños
y en el agua la vayan hundiendo,
para ver si en la noche estrellada
a muy lejos la llevan los vientos.

"As he went by he looked at me with a smile,
and he left me a star here inside."

"Where do you keep that star?"
a mischievous little boy asked.

"Has it gone out," others asked,
"like something under a magic charm?"

"No, children, the star is shining,
for I have it planted in my soul."

"What are stars down here like?"

"Child, just like in the sky."

"Go on, go on, old neighbor.
"Where was the glorious traveler headed?"

"His trail was lost in those mountains,
with my white doves and my dog.
But he left my house filled
with rose and jasmine bushes,
and the green grapes on the vine
ripened, and I found my granary
full the next morning.
All the doing of the good Apostle."

"What good luck you had, neighbor!"
two voices admonish at the same time.

The little ones are already asleep
and the fields are in deep silence.

Little children, think about Saint James
on the hazy roads of dreams!

Bright night of late July!
Saint James has passed by in the sky!
The sadness in my soul
I abandon on the white road,
to see whether the children find it
and might sink it in the water,
to see whether in the starry night
the winds carry it very far away.

El diamante

Noviembre de 1920
(Granada)

El diamante de una estrella
ha rayado el hondo cielo,
pájaro de luz que quiere
escapar del universo
y huye del enorme nido
donde estaba prisionero
sin saber que lleva atada
una cadena en el cuello.

Cazadores extrahumanos
están cazando luceros,
cisnes de plata maciza
en el agua del silencio.

Los chopos niños recitan
su cartilla; es el maestro
un chopo antiguo que mueve
tranquilo sus brazos muertos.
Ahora en el monte lejano
jugarán todos los muertos
a la baraja. ¡Es tan triste
la vida en el cementerio!

¡Rana, empieza tu cantar!
¡Grillo, sal de tu agujero!
Haced un bosque sonoro
con vuestras flautas. Yo vuelvo
hacia mi casa intranquilo.

Se agitan en mi cerebro
dos palomas campesinas
y en el horizonte, ¡lejos!,
se hunde el arcaduz del día.
¡Terrible noria del tiempo!

The Diamond

November 1920
(Granada)

The diamond of a star
has scratched the lofty sky,
a bird of light trying
to escape from the universe
and fleeing from the enormous nest
where it was held prisoner,
unaware that it has a chain
tied to its neck.

Superhuman huntsmen
are hunting evening-stars,
swans of solid silver
on the waters of silence.

The young black-poplars are reciting
from their primers; the teacher is
an ancient black-poplar waving
its dead arms peacefully.
Now on the distant mountain
all the dead are probably playing
cards. It's so dull,
life in the cemetery!

Frog, begin your song!
Cricket, come out of your hole!
Make the woods resound
with your flutes. I'm returning
homeward in agitation.

In my brain two wild pigeons
are thrashing about,
and on the horizon—far away!—
the day's bucket is sinking.
Fearful waterwheel of time!

Cantos nuevos

Agosto de 1920
(Vega de Zujaira)

Dice la tarde:
«¡Tengo sed de sombra!»
Dice la luna: «Yo, sed de luceros».
La fuente cristalina pide labios
y suspiros el viento.

Yo tengo sed de aromas y de risas.
Sed de cantares nuevos
sin lunas y sin lirios,
y sin amores muertos.

Un cantar de mañana que estremezca
a los remansos quietos
del porvenir. Y llene de esperanza
sus ondas y sus cienos.

Un cantar luminoso y reposado,
pleno de pensamiento,
virginal de tristezas y de angustias
y virginal de ensueños.

Cantar sin carne lírica que llene
de risas el silencio.
(Una bandada de palomas ciegas
lanzadas al misterio.)

Cantar que vaya al alma de las cosas
y al alma de los vientos
y que descanse al fin en la alegría
del corazón eterno.

Alba

Abril de 1919
(Granada)

Mi corazón oprimido
siente junto a la alborada
el dolor de sus amores

New Songs

August 1920
(Vega de Zujaira)

The afternoon says:
> "I'm thirsty for shade!"
The moon said: "And I, for evening-stars."
The crystal fountain asks for lips
and the wind for sighs.

I am thirsty for fragrances and laughter.
Thirsty for new songs
without moons or irises,
and without dead loves.

A morning song that can stir up
the still pools
of the future. And can fill with hope
its waters and its mud.

A luminous, restful song,
full of thought,
unsullied by sadness and anxiety
and unsullied by daydreams.

A song devoid of lyrical flesh, one that can fill
the silence with laughter.
(A flock of blind doves
flung into the mystery.)

A song that can penetrate the soul of things
and the soul of the winds
and that can finally rest in the joy
of the eternal heart.

Dawn

April 1919
(Granada)

My burdened heart
feels, alongside the aubade,
the pain of its loves

y el sueño de las distancias.
La luz de la aurora lleva
semilleros de nostalgias
y la tristeza sin ojos
de la médula del alma.
La gran tumba de la noche
su negro velo levanta
para ocultar con el día
la inmensa cumbre estrellada.

   ¿Qué haré yo sobre estos campos
cogiendo nidos y ramas,
rodeado de la aurora
y llena de noche el alma?
¿Qué haré si tienes tus ojos
muertos a las luces claras
y no ha de sentir mi carne
el calor de tus miradas?
¿Por qué te perdí por siempre
en aquella tarde clara?
Hoy mi pecho está reseco
como una estrella apagada.

Balada de un día de julio

Julio de 1919

   Esquilones de plata
llevan los bueyes.

   –¿Dónde vas, niña mía,
de sol y nieve?

   –Voy a las margaritas
del prado verde.

   –El prado está muy lejos
y miedo tiene.

   –Al airón y a la sombra
mi amor no teme.

and the dream of faraway places.
The light of dawn brings
seedbeds of nostalgia
and the eyeless sorrow
of the soul's marrow.
The great grave of night
lifts its black veil
to hide, by means of the day,
the immense starry summit.

What am I to do in these fields
collecting nests and branches,
surrounded by the dawn
while my soul is full of night?
What shall I do if your eyes are
dead to the bright light
and my flesh will not feel
the warmth of your glances?
Why did I lose you forever
on that bright afternoon?
Today my breast is parched
like an extinct star.

Ballad of a July Day

July 1919

The oxen wear
big silver collar-bells.

"Where are you going, my girl,
fashioned of sun and snow?"

"I'm going to the daisies
in the green meadow."

"The meadow is very far,
and contains fearful things."

"My love has no fear
of strong gusts[7] or shadow."

---

7. A conjecture, taking *airón* as an augmentative of *aire;* it normally means "heron" or "aigrette."

—Teme al sol, niña mía,
de sol y nieve.
—Se fue de mis cabellos
ya para siempre.
—¿Quién eres, blanca niña?
¿De dónde vienes?
—Vengo de los amores
y de las fuentes.

Esquilones de plata
llevan los bueyes.

—¿Qué llevas en la boca
que se te enciende?
—La estrella de mi amante
que vive y muere.
—¿Qué llevas en el pecho
tan fino y leve?
—La espada de mi amante
que vive y muere.
—¿Qué llevas en los ojos,
negro y solemne?
—Mi pensamiento triste
que siempre hiere.
—¿Por qué llevas un manto
negro de muerte?
—¡Ay, yo soy la viudita,
triste y sin bienes,
del conde del Laurel
de los Laureles!

—¿A quién buscas aquí
si a nadie quieres?
—Busco el cuerpo del conde
de los Laureles.

"Fear the sun, my girl,
fashioned of sun and snow."

"By now it has fled from my hair
forever."

"Who are you, lily-white girl?
Where do you come from?"

"I come from loves
and from fountains."

The oxen wear
big silver collar-bells.

"What do you have on your lips
that makes them blaze so?"

"The star of my lover,
living and dying."

"What do you have on your bosom
so fine and light?"

"The sword of my lover,
living and dying."

"What do you have in your eyes
that is so dark and solemn?"

"My sad thoughts,
which always wound me."

"Why do you wear a mantle
deathly black?"

"Ah, I'm the young widow,
sad and without possessions,
of the Count del Laurel
de los Laureles!"[8]

"Whom are you seeking here
if you love no one?"

"I'm seeking the body of the Count
de los Laureles."

---

8. A reference to another children's game, frequently cited in Lorca's works, and also mentioned in *Platero y yo* (Platero and I; 1917) by Juan Ramón Jiménez.

–¿Tú buscas el amor,
viudita aleve?
Tú buscas un amor
que ojalá encuentres.

–Estrellitas del cielo
son mis quereres.
¿Dónde hallaré a mi amante
que vive y muere?

–Está muerto en el agua,
niña de nieve,
cubierto de nostalgias
y de claveles.

–¡Ay, caballero errante
de los cipreses!
Una noche de luna
mi alma te ofrece.

–¡Ah Isis soñadora!,
niña sin mieles,
la que en bocas de niños
su cuento vierte.
Mi corazón te ofrezco,
corazón tenue,
herido por los ojos
de las mujeres.

–Caballero galante,
con Dios te quedes.
Voy a buscar al conde
de los Laureles . . .

–Adiós, mi doncellita,
rosa durmiente,
tú vas para el amor
y yo a la muerte.

Esquilones de plata
llevan los bueyes.

Mi corazón desangra
como una fuente.

"You're seeking love,
treacherous young widow?
You're seeking a love
which I hope you find."

"The little stars in the sky
are my loves.
Where will I find my lover,
living and dying?"

"He lies dead in the water,
girl of snow,
covered with nostalgia
and carnations."

"Alas, knight errant
of the cypresses!
My soul offers you
a moonlight night."

"Ah, dreaming Isis,
girl without honey,
girl who pours her story
into children's mouths!
I offer you my heart,
a delicate heart,
wounded by the eyes
of women."

"Gallant knight,
go your own way.
I'm off to seek the Count
de los Laureles." . . .

"Farewell, my young damsel,
sleeping rose,
you are headed for love
and I for death."

The oxen wear
big silver collar-bells.

My heart is bleeding
like a fountain.

Sueño

Mayo de 1919

Mi corazón reposa junto a la fuente fría.

    (Llénala con tus hilos,
    araña del olvido.)

El agua de la fuente su canción le decía.

    (Llénala con tus hilos,
    araña del olvido.)

Mi corazón despierto sus amores decía.

    (Araña del silencio,
    téjele tu misterio.)

El agua de la fuente lo escuchaba sombría.

    (Araña del silencio,
    téjele tu misterio.)

Mi corazón se vuelca sobre la fuente fría.

    (Manos blancas, lejanas,
    detened a las aguas.)

Y el agua se lo lleva cantando de alegría.

    (¡Manos blancas, lejanas,
    nada queda en las aguas!)

La veleta yacente

Diciembre de 1920
(Madrid)

    El duro corazón de la veleta
entre el libro del tiempo.
(Una hoja la tierra
y otra hoja el cielo.)
Aplastóse doliente sobre letras
de tejados viejos.
Lírica flor de torre
y luna de los vientos,
abandona el estambre de la cruz

Dream

May 1919

My heart reposes beside the cold fountain.

> (Fill the fountain with your threads,
> spider of oblivion.)

The water of the fountain sang it its song.

> (Fill it with your threads,
> spider of oblivion.)

My waking heart told its loves.

> (Spider of silence,
> weave your mystery for it.)

The water of the fountain listened to it somberly.

> (Spider of silence,
> weave your mystery for it.)

My heart overturns onto the cold fountain.

> (White, distant hands,
> hold back the waters.)

And the water carries it off, singing with joy.

> (White, distant hands,
> nothing is left in the waters!)

The Weather Vane on the Ground

December 1920

(Madrid)

    The hard heart of the weather vane
within the book of time.
(One leaf the earth
and another leaf the sky.)
It crashed down painfully onto the writing
of old roofs.
Lyrical tower-blossom
and moon of the winds,
it forsakes the stamen of the cross

y dispersa sus pétalos,
para caer sobre las losas frías
comida por la oruga
de los ecos.
Yaces bajo una acacia.
¡Memento!
No podías latir
porque eras de hierro . . .
Mas poseíste la forma,
¡conténtate con eso!
Y húndete bajo el verde
légamo,
en busca de tu gloria
de fuego,
aunque te llamen tristes
las torres desde lejos
y oigas en las veletas
chirriar tus compañeros.
Húndete bajo el paño
verdoso de tu lecho,
que ni la blanca monja,
ni el perro,
ni la luna menguante,
ni el lucero,
ni el turbio sacristán
del convento,
recordarán tus gritos
del invierno.
Húndete lentamente,
que si no, luego,
te llevarán los hombres
de los trapos viejos.
Y ojalá pudiera darte
por compañero
este corazón mío
¡tan incierto!

and scatters its petals,
to fall onto the cold flagstones,
gnawed by the caterpillar
of echoes.

   You are lying under an acacia.
"Remember thou art mortal!"
You were unable to have a heartbeat
because you were made of iron . . .
But you possessed form,
be satisfied with that!
And sink beneath the green
slime,
in quest of your fiery
glory,
though you are summoned sadly
by the towers from afar
and you hear in the weather vanes
creaking companions.
Sink beneath the greenish
cloth of your bed,
for neither the white-clad nun,
nor the dog,
nor the waning moon,
nor the evening-star,
nor the muddled sacristan
of the monastery
will recall your cries
of wintertime.
Sink slowly,
or else very soon
you'll be carried away
by the ragpickers.
And how I wish I could give you
as a companion
this heart of mine
which is so full of doubts!

Corazón nuevo

Junio de 1918

(Granada)

Mi corazón, como una sierpe,
se ha desprendido de su piel,
y aquí la miro entre mis dedos,
llena de heridas y de miel.

Los pensamientos que anidaron
en tus arrugas ¿dónde están?
¿Dónde las rosas que aromaron
a Jesucristo y a Satán?

¡Pobre envoltura que ha oprimido
a mi fantástico lucero!
Gris pergamino dolorido
de lo que quise y ya no quiero.

Yo veo en ti fetos de ciencias,
momias de versos y esqueletos
de mis antiguas inocencias
y mis románticos secretos.

¿Te colgaré sobre los muros
de mi museo sentimental,
junto a los gélidos y oscuros
lirios durmientes de mi mal?

¿O te pondré sobre los pinos
—libro doliente de mi amor—
para que sepas de los trinos
que da a la aurora el ruiseñor?

Se ha puesto el sol

Agosto de 1920

Se ha puesto el sol.
                    Los árboles
meditan como estatuas.
Ya está el trigo segado.
¡Qué tristeza
de las norias paradas!

New Heart

June 1918
(Granada)

My heart, like a snake,
has sloughed off its skin,
which I look at here in my fingers,
full of wounds and honey.

The thoughts that nested
in your wrinkles, where are they?
Where are the roses that perfumed
Jesus Christ and Satan?

Poor wrapping which burdened
my imaginary evening-star!
Gray, pain-filled parchment
of what I loved but no longer love.

I see in you fetuses of knowledge,
mummies of poetry and skeletons
of my former innocence
and my romantic secrets.

Shall I hang you on the walls
of my museum of emotions,
next to the dark, frozen
sleeping irises of my illness?

Or shall I place you on the pines—
aching book of my love—
so you can hear news of the warbling
that the nightingale gives the dawn?

The Sun Has Set

August 1920

The sun has set.
                    The trees
meditate like statues.
The wheat has now been harvested.
How sad
the stationary waterwheels are!

Un perro campesino
quiere comerse a Venus, y le ladra.
Brilla sobre su campo de pre-beso,
como una gran manzana.

Los mosquitos –pegasos del rocío–
vuelan, el aire en calma.
La Penélope inmensa de la luz
teje una noche clara.

«Hijas mías, dormid, que viene el lobo»,
las ovejitas balan.
«¿Ha llegado el otoño, compañeras?»,
dice una flor ajada.

¡Ya vendrán los pastores con sus nidos
por la sierra lejana!
Ya jugarán las niñas en la puerta
de la vieja posada,
y habrá coplas de amor
que ya se saben
de memoria las casas.

Pajarita de papel

Julio de 1920

¡Oh pajarita de papel!
Águila de los niños.
Con las plumas de letras,
sin palomo
y sin nido.

Las manos aún mojadas de misterio
te crean en un frío
anochecer de otoño, cuando mueren
los pájaros y el ruido
de la lluvia nos hace amar la lámpara,
el corazón y el libro.

Naces para vivir unos minutos
en el frágil castillo
de naipes, que se eleva tembloroso
como el tallo de un lirio,

A rural dog
wants to eat Venus, and barks at it.
It shines upon its pre-kiss field
like a big apple.

The gnats—Pegasuses of the dew—
are flying, the air is calm.
The immense Penelope of light
is weaving a clear night.

"Go to sleep, children, or the wolf will come,"
the little sheep bleat.
"Has fall arrived, friends?"
asks a faded flower.

Now the shepherds with their nests will come
down the distant mountain range!
Now the girls will play in the doorway
of the old inn,
and there will be love songs
which the houses
already know by heart.

Paper Bird

July 1920

O folded-paper bird!
The children's eagle.
With feathers of printed paper,
without a cock-pigeon
and without a nest.

Hands still moist with mystery
create you at a cold
autumnal nightfall, when the birds
die and the noise
of the rain makes us love the lamp,
the heart, and the book.

You are born to live a few minutes
in the fragile house
of cards, which rises tremblingly
like the stalk of an iris,

y meditas allí, ciega y sin alas,
que pudiste haber sido
el atleta grotesco que sonríe
ahorcado por un hilo,
el barco silencioso sin remeros ni velamen,
el lírico
buque fantasma del miedoso insecto,
o el triste borriquito
que escarnecen, haciéndolo pegaso,
los soplos de los niños.

Pero en medio de tu meditación
van gotas de humorismo.
Hecha con la corteza de la ciencia
te ríes del destino,
y gritas: «Blancaflor no muere nunca,
ni se muere Luisito.
La mañana es eterna, es eterna
la fuente del rocío.»

Y aunque no crees en nada dices esto,
no se enteren los niños
de que hay sombra detrás de las estrellas
y sombra en tu castillo.

En medio de la mesa, al derrumbarse
tu azul mansión, has visto
que el milano te mira ansiosamente:
es un recién nacido.
Una pompa de espuma sobre el agua
del sufrimiento vivo.

Y tú vas a sus labios luminosos
mientras ríen los niños,
y callan los papás, no sea despierten
los dolores vecinos.

Así, pájaro clown, desapareces
para nacer en otro sitio.
Así, pájaro esfinge, das tu alma
de ave fénix al limbo.

and there you meditate, blind and wingless,
that you might have been
a grotesque smiling athlete
hanged by a thread;
or the silent vessel without oarsmen or sails,
the operatic
Flying Dutchman's ship of the timorous insect;
or the sad little burro
mocked, as they make him a Pegasus,
by the children's blowing.

But amid your meditation
there are drops of humor.
Constructed from the cortex of knowledge,
you laugh at destiny,
shouting: "Blancaflor never dies,
nor does Luisito.[9]
Morning is eternal, eternal as
the source of the dew."

And, though you believe in nothing, you say this
so the children won't become aware
that there is darkness behind the stars
and darkness in your house of cards.

In the middle of the table, when your blue mansion
tumbled down, you saw
the hawk gazing at you nervously:
"He's a new-born babe.
A bubble of foam on the waters
of vivid suffering."

And you go to his bright lips
while the children laugh,
and their daddies keep silent, so as not to awaken
griefs close at hand.

Thus, clown-bird, you disappear
to be born elsewhere.
Thus, sphinx-bird, you give your
phoenix-soul to limbo.

---

9. Presumably, heroes of stories for children.

Madrigal

Octubre de 1920
(Madrid)

Mi beso era una granada,
profunda y abierta;
tu boca era rosa
de papel.
El fondo un campo de nieve.

Mis manos eran hierros
para los yunques;
tu cuerpo era el ocaso
de una campanada.
El fondo un campo de nieve.

En la agujereada
calavera azul
hicieron estalactitas
mis te quiero.
El fondo un campo de nieve.

Llenáronse de moho
mis sueños infantiles,
y taladró a la luna
mi dolor salomónico.
El fondo un campo de nieve.

Ahora amaestro grave
a la alta escuela,
a mi amor y a mis sueños
(caballitos sin ojos).
Y el fondo es un campo de nieve.

Una campana

Octubre de 1920

Una campana serena,
crucificada en su ritmo,
define a la mañana

Madrigal

October 1920
(Madrid)

My kiss was a pomegranate,
deep and open;
your lips were a paper
rose.

The backdrop, a snowy field.

My hands were chunks of iron
for anvils;
your body was the sunset
of a ringing church bell.

The backdrop, a snowy field.

In the perforated
blue skull
my repeated "I love you"
formed stalactites.

The backdrop, a snowy field.

The dreams of my childhood
were covered with mold,
and my spirally twisted grief
drilled through the moon.

The backdrop, a snowy field.

Now, in all seriousness, I train,
in a school of advanced horsemanship,
my love and my dreams
(little eyeless horses).

And the backdrop is a snowy field.

A Church Bell

October 1920

A serene church bell,
crucified on its cadence,
defines the morning

con peluca de niebla
y arroyos de lágrimas.
Mi viejo chopo,
turbio de ruiseñores,
esperaba
poner entre las hierbas
sus ramas
mucho antes que el otoño
lo dorara.
Pero los puntales
de mis miradas
lo sostenían.
¡Viejo chopo, aguarda!
¿No sientes la madera
de mi amor desgarrada?
Tiéndete en la pradera
cuando cruja mi alma,
que un vendaval de besos
y palabras
ha dejado rendida,
lacerada.

Consulta

Agosto de 1920

¡Pasionaria azul!,
yunque de mariposas.
¿Vives bien en el limo
de las horas?

(¡Oh poeta infantil,
quiebra tu reloj!)

Clara estrella azul,
ombligo de la aurora.
¿Vives bien en la espuma
de la sombra?

(¡Oh poeta infantil,
quiebra tu reloj!)

Corazón azulado,
lámpara de mi alcoba.

with a wig of mist
and brooks of tears.
My old black-poplar,
in a confusion of nightingales,
had been expecting
to lower its branches
into the grass
long before autumn
gilded it.
But the props
of my glances
were holding it up.
Old black-poplar, wait!
Don't you sense the lacerated
timber of my love?
Stretch out on the meadow
when my soul crackles, my soul,
which a gale of kisses
and words
has left exhausted,
torn apart.

Consultation

August 1920

Blue passionflower,
anvil for butterflies!
Is your life comfortable in the moist soil
of the hours?

(O child-poet,
smash your watch!)

Bright blue star,
navel of the dawn.
Is your life comfortable in the foam
of shadow?

(O child-poet,
smash your watch!)

Bluish heart,
lamp of my bedroom.

¿Lates bien sin mi sangre
filarmónica?

(¡Oh poeta infantil,
quiebra tu reloj!)

Os comprendo y me dejo
arrumbado en la cómoda
al insecto del tiempo.
Sus metálicas gotas
no se oirán en la calma
de mi alcoba.
Me dormiré tranquilo
como dormís vosotras,
pasionarias y estrellas,
que al fin la mariposa
volará en la corriente
de las horas
mientras nace en mi tronco
la rosa.

Tarde

Noviembre de 1919

Tarde lluviosa en gris cansado,
y sigue el caminar.
Los árboles marchitos.
                        Mi cuarto, solitario.
Y los retratos viejos
y el libro sin cortar . . .

Chorrea la tristeza por los muebles
y por mi alma.
            Quizá,
no tenga para mí Naturaleza
el pecho de cristal.

Y me duele la carne del corazón
y la carne del alma.
            Y al hablar,
se quedan mis palabras en el aire
como corchos sobre agua.

Are you beating properly without my
music-loving blood?

 (O child-poet,
smash your watch!)

 I understand you all, and I leave myself,
discarded in the chest-of-drawers,
to the insect of time.
Its metallic dripping
won't be heard in the calm
of my bedroom.
I shall fall asleep tranquilly
the way that you sleep,
passionflowers and stars,
because finally the butterfly
will fly on the current
of the hours
while the rose
sprouts from my torso.

Afternoon

November 1919

 Rainy afternoon in tired gray,
and the journey goes on.
The trees, faded.
     My room, lonely.
And the old portraits
and the book still uncut . . .

 Sadness flows down the furniture
and down my soul.
     Perhaps
Nature doesn't have
a glass bosom for me.

 And the flesh of my heart hurts me,
and the flesh of my soul.
     And when I speak,
my words remain in the air
like corks on water.

Sólo por tus ojos
sufro yo este mal,
tristezas de antaño
y las que vendrán.

Tarde lluviosa en gris cansado,
y sigue el caminar.

"Hay almas que tienen . . ."

8 de febrero de 1920

Hay almas que tienen
azules luceros,
mañanas marchitas
entre hojas del tiempo,
y castos rincones
que guardan un viejo
rumor de nostalgias
y sueños.

Otras almas tienen
dolientes espectros
de pasiones. Frutas
con gusanos. Ecos
de una voz quemada
que viene de lejos
como una corriente
de sombra. Recuerdos
vacíos de llanto,
y migajas de besos.

Mi alma está madura
hace mucho tiempo,
y se desmorona
turbia de misterio.
Piedras juveniles,
roídas de ensueño,
caen sobre las aguas
de mis pensamientos.
Cada piedra dice:
«¡Dios está muy lejos!»

Only because of your eyes
do I suffer this ailment,
sadnesses of yesteryear
and those to come.

Rainy afternoon in tired gray,
and the journey goes on.

"There are souls which have . . ."

February 8, 1920

There are souls which have
blue evening-stars,
faded mornings
between pages of time,
and chaste corners
preserving an old
sound of nostalgia
and dreams.

Other souls have
painful ghosts
of passions. Fruit
with worms. Echoes
of a burnt voice
coming from afar
like a current
of shadow. Empty
memories of weeping,
and crumbs of kisses.

My soul has been ripe
for some time,
and is crumbling
in a confusion of mystery.
Juvenile stones,
eroded by daydreaming,
fall into the waters
of my thoughts.
Each stone says:
"God is very far!"

Prólogo

24 de julio de 1920
(Vega de Zujaira)

Mi corazón está aquí,
Dios mío.
Hunde tu cetro en él, Señor.
Es un membrillo
demasiado otoñal
y está podrido.
Arranca los esqueletos
de los gavilanes líricos
que tanto, tanto lo hirieron,
y si acaso tienes pico
móndale su corteza
de Hastío.

Mas si no quieres hacerlo,
me da lo mismo,
guárdate tu cielo azul,
que es tan aburrido,
el rigodón de los astros
y tu Infinito,
que yo pediré prestado
el corazón a un amigo.
Un corazón con arroyos
y pinos,
y un ruiseñor de hierro
que resista
el martillo
de los siglos.

Además, Satanás me quiere mucho,
fue compañero mío
en un examen de
lujuria, y el pícaro
buscará a Margarita
—me lo tiene ofrecido—,
Margarita morena,
sobre un fondo de viejos olivos,
con dos trenzas de noche
de Estío,

Prologue

July 24, 1920
(Vega de Zujaira)

Here is my heart,
God.
Plunge your scepter into it, Lord.
It's a quince
that ripened too late in fall
and is rotten.
Tear out the skeletons
of the lyrical sparrow hawks
that have wounded it so, so badly,
and if you happen to have a beak,
peel away its rind
of Disgust.

But if you don't wish to do so,
it's all the same to me.
Keep your blue sky,
which is so boring,
the rigadoon of the planets,
and your Infinity,
for I shall borrow
a heart from a friend.
A heart with streams
and pines,
and an iron nightingale
which can withstand
the hammer
of the centuries.

Besides, Satan loves me very much,
he was my companion
at an exam on
lustfulness, and the scoundrel
will look for Margarete
(he has made me that offer),
a dark-skinned Margarete,
against a setting of old olive trees,
with two braids like
a summer night,

para que yo desgarre
sus muslos limpios.
Y entonces, ¡oh Señor!,
seré tan rico
o más que tú,
porque el vacío
no puede compararse
al vino
con que Satán obsequia
a sus buenos amigos.
Licor hecho con llanto.
¡Qué más da!
Es lo mismo
que tu licor compuesto
de trinos.

   Dime, Señor,
¡Dios mío!
¿Nos hundes en la sombra
del abismo?
¿Somos pájaros ciegos
sin nidos?

   La luz se va apagando.
¿Y el aceite divino?
Las olas agonizan.
¿Has querido
jugar como si fuéramos
soldaditos?
Dime, Señor,
¡Dios mío!
¿No llega el dolor nuestro
a tus oídos?
¿No han hecho las blasfemias
babeles sin ladrillos
para herirte, o te gustan
los gritos?
¿Estás sordo? ¿Estás ciego?
¿O eres bizco
de espíritu
y ves el alma humana
con tonos invertidos?

so I can lacerate
her chaste thighs.
And then, Lord,
I'll be just as rich
as you, or more so,
because the void
can't be compared
to the wine
which Satan presents
to his good friends.
A beverage made with tears.
What of it?
It's the same
as your beverage compounded
of warbling.

Tell me, Lord,
my God!
Do you plunge us into the shadow
of the abyss?
Are we blind birds
without nests?

The light is going out.
And the sacred oil?
The waves are dying.
Was it your intention
to play as if we were
toy soldiers?
Tell me, Lord,
my God!
Doesn't our sorrow reach
your ears?
Haven't our blasphemies built
brickless towers of Babel
to wound you, or do you like
mournful cries?
Are you deaf? Are you blind?
Or are you mentally
crosseyed,
so that you see the human soul
in inverted images?

¡Oh Señor soñoliento!
¡Mira mi corazón
frío
como un membrillo
demasiado otoñal
que está podrido!

Si tu luz va a llegar,
abre los ojos vivos,
pero si continúas
dormido,
ven, Satanás errante,
sangriento peregrino,
ponme la Margarita
morena en los olivos,
con las trenzas de noche
de Estío,
que yo sabré encenderle
sus ojos pensativos
con mis besos manchados
de lirios.
Y oiré una tarde ciega
mi «¡Enrique! ¡Enrique!»
lírico,
mientras todos mis sueños
se llenan de rocío.

Aquí, Señor, te dejo
mi corazón antiguo,
voy a pedir prestado
otro nuevo a un amigo.
Corazón con arroyos
y pinos.
Corazón sin culebras
ni lirios.
Robusto, con la gracia
de un joven campesino,
que atraviesa de un salto
el río.

O drowsy Lord!
Look at my heart,
which is as cold
as a quince
that ripened too late in fall
and is rotten!

If your light is to come,
open your living eyes,
but if you go on
sleeping,
come, errant Satan,
blood-stained pilgrim,
place a dark-skinned Margarete
among the olive trees for me,
with her braids like
a summer night,
for I will be able to ignite
her pensive eyes
with my kisses stained
with irises.
And, one blind evening, I shall hear
the "Heinrich! Heinrich!" meant for me,
so operatic,
while all my dreams
are filled with dew.

Here, Lord, I leave you
my former heart,
I'm going to borrow
a new one from a friend.
A heart with streams
and pines.
A heart without snakes
or irises.
A robust one, with the gracefulness
of a young country lad
who crosses the river
with one jump.

Balada interior

16 de julio de 1920
(Vega de Zujaira)

A Gabriel

El corazón
que tenía en la escuela,
donde estuvo pintada
la cartilla primera,
¿está en ti,
noche negra?

(Frío, frío,
como el agua
del río.)

El primer beso
que supo a beso y fue
para mis labios niños
como la lluvia fresca,
¿está en ti,
noche negra?

(Frío, frío,
como el agua
del río.)

Mi primer verso,
la niña de las trenzas
que miraba de frente,
¿está en ti,
noche negra?

(Frío, frío,
como el agua
del río.)

Pero mi corazón
roído de culebras,
el que estuvo colgado
del árbol de la ciencia,
¿está en ti,
noche negra?

Inward Ballad

July 16, 1920

(Vega de Zujaira)

To Gabriel

The heart
I had when in school,
where my first primer
was painted,
is it in you,
black night?

(Cold, cold,
like the water
in the river.)

The first kiss
that tasted like a kiss, and was
to my childish lips
like the fresh rain,
is it in you,
black night?

(Cold, cold,
like the water
in the river.)

My first line of verse,
the girl with braids
who always looked straight ahead,
are they in you,
black night?

(Cold, cold,
like the water
in the river.)

But my heart,
gnawed by serpents,
the heart that once hung
from the Tree of Knowledge,
is it in you,
black night?

(Caliente, caliente,
como el agua
de la fuente.)

Mi amor errante,
castillo sin firmeza,
de sombras enmohecidas,
¿está en ti,
noche negra?

(Caliente, caliente,
como el agua
de la fuente.)

¡Oh gran dolor!
Admites en tu cueva
nada más que la sombra.
¿Es cierto,
noche negra?

(Caliente, caliente,
como el agua
de la fuente.)

¡Oh corazón perdido!
¡Requiem aeternam!

El lagarto viejo

26 de julio de 1920
(Vega de Zujaira)

En la agostada senda
he visto al buen lagarto
(gota de cocodrilo)
meditando.
Con su verde levita
de abate del diablo,
su talante correcto
y su cuello planchado,
tiene un aire muy triste
de viejo catedrático.
¡Esos ojos marchitos
de artista fracasado

(Hot, hot,
like the water
from the spring.)

My wandering love,
an insecure castle
with moldy shadows,
is it in you,
black night?

(Hot, hot,
like the water
from the spring.)

O great pain!
You admit to your cave
shadow alone.
Isn't that true,
black night?

(Hot, hot,
like the water
from the spring.)

O lost heart!
Requiem aeternam!

The Old Lizard

July 26, 1920
(Vega de Zujaira)

On the withered path
I have seen the good lizard
(a drop-size crocodile)
meditating.
With his green frock coat
like that worn by an abbot of the devil,
his proper bearing,
and his ironed collar,
he has the very sad appearance
of an old professor.
Those faded eyes
of a failed artist,

cómo miran la tarde
desmayada!

¿Es éste su paseo
crepuscular, amigo?
Usad bastón, ya estáis
muy viejo, Don Lagarto,
y los niños del pueblo
pueden daros un susto.
¿Qué buscáis en la senda,
filósofo cegato,
si el fantasma indeciso
de la tarde agosteña
ha roto el horizonte?

¿Buscáis la azul limosna
del cielo moribundo?
¿Un céntimo de estrella?
¿O acaso
estudiasteis un libro
de Lamartine, y os gustan
los trinos platerescos
de los pájaros?

(Miras al sol poniente,
y tus ojos relucen,
¡oh dragón de las ranas!,
con un fulgor humano.
Las góndolas sin remos
de las ideas, cruzan
el agua tenebrosa
de tus iris quemados.)

¿Venís quizá en la busca
de la bella lagarta,
verde como los trigos
de Mayo,
como las cabelleras
de las fuentes dormidas,
que os despreciaba, y luego
se fue de vuestro campo?
¡Oh dulce idilio roto
sobre la fresca juncia!

how they gaze at the swooning
afternoon!

Is this your[10] twilight
stroll, friend?
You use a cane; you're already
very old, Mister Lizard,
and the village children
can throw a scare into you.
What are you seeking on the path,
nearsighted philosopher?
To see whether the undecided ghost
of the August afternoon
has torn the horizon?

Are you seeking the blue alms
of the dying sky?
A star-penny?
Or, by chance,
have you studied a book
by Lamartine, and do you like
the plateresque warbling
of the birds?

(You gaze at the setting sun,
and your eyes glisten,
O dragon to frogs,
with a human glow.
The oarless gondolas
of thought furrow
the shadowy waters
of your scorched pupils.)

Have you perhaps come in quest
of the lovely lady-lizard,
green as wheatfields
in May,
as the heads of hair
of the sleeping fountains,
the lady who scorned you and then
departed from your field?
O the sweet idyll
on the cool rushes—now shattered!

10. In this poem, Lorca uses all three forms of address for "you."

¡Pero vivir!, ¡qué diantre!
Me habéis sido simpático.
El lema de «me opongo
a la serpiente» triunfa
en esa gran papada
de arzobispo cristiano.

Ya se ha disuelto el sol
en la copa del monte,
y enturbian el camino
los rebaños.
Es hora de marcharse,
dejad la angosta senda
y no continuéis
meditando,
que lugar tendréis luego
de mirar las estrellas
cuando os coman sin prisa
los gusanos.

¡Volved a vuestra casa
bajo el pueblo de grillos!
¡Buenas noches, amigo
Don Lagarto!

Ya está el campo sin gente,
los montes apagados
y el camino desierto.
Sólo de cuando en cuando
canta un cuco en la umbría
de los álamos.

Patio húmedo

1920

Las arañas
iban por los laureles.

La casualidad
se va tornando en nieve,
y los años dormidos
ya se atreven

But we must go on living! What the devil!
I've found you congenial.
The motto "I set myself against
the Serpent" is triumphant
in your big dewlap,
like a Christian archbishop's.

   Now the sun has dissolved
in the mountain's summit-goblet,
and the flocks
are confusing the road.
It's time to depart;
leave the narrow path
and don't go on
meditating,
for you'll have plenty of time
to gaze at the stars
when the worms
eat you unhurriedly.

   Return to your house
under the crickets' village!
Good night, my friend,
Mister Lizard!

   The field is now free of people,
the mountains extinguished,
and the road deserted.
Only, every so often,
a cuckoo calls in the shade
of the poplars.

Damp Patio

1920

   The spiders
were crawling on the laurels.

   Chance
is turning into snow,
and the sleeping years
now venture

a clavar los telares
del siempre.

La Quietud hecha esfinge
se ríe de la Muerte
que canta melancólica
en un grupo
de lejanos cipreses.

La yedra de las gotas
tapiza las paredes
empapadas de arcaicos
misereres.

¡Oh torre vieja!
Llora
tus lágrimas mudéjares
sobre este grave patio
que no tiene fuente.

Las arañas
iban por los laureles.

Balada de la placeta

1919

Cantan los niños
en la noche quieta:
¡Arroyo claro,
fuente serena!

Los niños
¿Qué tiene tu divino
corazón en fiesta?

Yo
Un doblar de campanas
perdidas en la niebla.

Los niños
Ya nos dejas cantando
en la plazuela.
¡Arroyo claro,
fuente serena!

to set up the looms
of always.

Quietude, turned into a sphinx,
laughs at Death,
which sings gloomily
in a group
of distant cypresses.

The ivy, full of drops,
carpets the walls,
which are steeped in archaic
Misereres.

O ancient tower!
           Weep
your Moorish-style tears
onto this solemn patio
that has no fountain.

The spiders
were crawling on the laurels.

Ballad of the Little Square

1919

The children sing
in the still night:
"Clear stream,
calm fountain!"

THE CHILDREN
   What makes your divine
heart keep holiday?

I
   A peal of church bells
lost in the mist.

THE CHILDREN
   Now you leave us singing
in the little square.
Clear stream,
calm fountain!

¿Qué tienes en tus manos
de primavera?

Yo
　Una rosa de sangre
y una azucena.

Los niños
　Mójalas en el agua
de la canción añeja.
¡Arroyo claro,
fuente serena!

　¿Qué sientes en tu boca
roja y sedienta?

Yo
　El sabor de los huesos
de mi gran calavera.

Los niños
　Bebe el agua tranquila
de la canción añeja.
¡Arroyo claro,
fuente serena!

　¿Por qué te vas tan lejos
de la plazuela?

Yo
　¡Voy en busca de magos
y de princesas!

Los niños
　¿Quién te enseñó el camino
de los poetas?

Yo
　La fuente y el arroyo
de la canción añeja.

Los niños
　¿Te vas lejos, muy lejos
del mar y de la tierra?

Yo
　Se ha llenado de luces

What is there in your springlike
hands?

I

A rose of blood
and a lily.

THE CHILDREN
Sprinkle them with the water
of the age-old song.
Bright stream,
calm fountain!

What do you taste in your
red, thirsty mouth?

I

The flavor of the bones
of my large skull.

THE CHILDREN
Drink the tranquil water
of the age-old song.
Bright stream,
calm fountain!

Why are you departing so far
from the little square?

I

I'm off in quest of wizards
and princesses!

THE CHILDREN
Who showed you the path
that poets take?

I

The fountain and stream
in the age-old song.

THE CHILDREN
Are you going far, very far
from the sea and the land?

I

My silken heart

mi corazón de seda,
de campanas perdidas,
de lirios y de abejas.

Y yo me iré muy lejos,
más allá de esas sierras,
más allá de los mares,
cerca de las estrellas,
para pedirle a Cristo
Señor que me devuelva
mi alma antigua de niño,
madura de leyendas,
con el gorro de plumas
y el sable de madera.

Los niños
Ya nos dejas cantando
en la plazuela:
¡Arroyo claro,
fuente serena!

Las pupilas enormes
de las frondas resecas,
heridas por el viento,
lloran las hojas muertas.

Encrucijada

Julio de 1920

¡Oh, qué dolor el tener
versos en la lejanía
de la pasión, y el cerebro
todo manchado de tinta!

¡Oh, qué dolor no tener
la fantástica camisa
del hombre feliz: la piel
–alfombra del sol– curtida!

(Alrededor de mis ojos
bandadas de letras giran.)

¡Oh, qué dolor el dolor
antiguo de la poesía,

has become full of lights,
of lost church bells,
of irises and bees.
And I shall go very far,
beyond those mountain ranges,
beyond the seas,
near the stars,
to ask Christ
the Lord to restore to me
my former childhood soul,
ripe with legend,
along with my plumed cap
and wooden saber.

THE CHILDREN
    Now you leave us singing
in the little square:
Bright stream,
calm fountain!

    The enormous pupils
of the parched fronds,
wounded by the wind,
weep for the dead leaves.

Crossroads

July 1920

    Oh, what grief to have
poetry in the far-off distance
of passion, and my brain
all ink-stained!

    Oh, what grief not to have
the fantasy shirt
of the happy man: my skin—
the sun's carpet—tanned!

    (All around my eyes
flocks of writing whirl.)

    Oh, what grief, the ancient
grief of poetry,

este dolor pegajoso
tan lejos del agua limpia!
¡Oh dolor de lamentarse
por sorber la vena lírica!
¡Oh dolor de fuente ciega
y molino sin harina!

¡Oh qué dolor no tener
dolor y pasar la vida
sobre la hierba incolora
de la vereda indecisa!

¡Oh el más profundo dolor,
el dolor de la alegría,
reja que nos abre surcos
donde el llanto fructifica!

(Por un monte de papel
asoma la luna fría.)
¡Oh dolor de la verdad!
¡Oh dolor de la mentira!

Hora de estrellas

1920

El silencio redondo de la noche
sobre el pentágrama
del infinito.

Yo me salgo desnudo a la calle,
maduro de versos
perdidos.
Lo negro, acribillado
por el canto del grillo,
tiene ese fuego fatuo,
muerto,
del sonido.
Esa luz musical
que percibe
el espíritu.

Los esqueletos de mil mariposas
duermen en mi recinto.

that contagious grief
so far from clear water!

Oh, the grief of lamenting
because you have imbibed the lyric vein!
Oh, the grief, like that of an obstructed fountain
or a flourless mill!

Oh, what grief not to have
grief, and to spend your life
on the colorless grass
of the undecided path!

Oh, that deepest grief,
the grief of joy,
a plowshare that opens furrows for us
where weeping germinates!

(Over a mountain of paper
the cold moon shows its face.)
Oh, the grief of truth!
Oh, the grief of falsehood!

Hour of Stars

1920

The total silence of the night
on the music-stave
of infinity.

I go out into the street naked,
ripe with lost
poetry.
The blackness, riddled
by the cricket's call,
possesses that dead
will-o'-the-wisp
of sound.
That musical light
which the spirit
perceives.

The skeletons of a thousand butterflies
sleep in my enclosure.

Hay una juventud de brisas locas
sobre el río.

El camino

No conseguirá nunca
tu lanza
herir al horizonte.
La montaña
es un escudo
que lo guarda.
No sueñes con la sangre de la luna
y descansa.
Pero deja, camino,
que mis plantas
exploren la caricia
de la rociada.

¡Quiromántico enorme!
¿Conocerás las almas
por el débil tatuaje
que olvidan en tu espalda?
Si eres un Flammarión
de las pisadas,
¡cómo debes amar
a los asnos que pasan
acariciando con ternura humilde
tu carne desgarrada!
Ellos solos meditan dónde puede
llegar tu enorme lanza.
Ellos solos, que son
los Bhudas de la Fauna,
cuando viejos y heridos deletrean
tu libro sin palabras.

¡Cuánta melancolía
tienes entre las casas
del poblado!
¡Qué clara

There is a crowd of wild young breezes
on the river.

The Road

Your lance
will never succeed
in wounding the horizon.
The mountain
is a shield
protecting it.

Don't dream of the moon's blood,
but rest.
Yet, road, let
my feet
explore the caress
of the shower.

Vast palm-reader!
Will you recognize the souls
by the faint tattoo
they negligently leave behind on your back?
If you're a Flammarion[11]
of footprints,
how you must love
the donkeys that go by
caressing your lacerated flesh
with humble tenderness!
They alone wonder how far
your enormous lance can reach.
They alone, who are
the Buddhas of the animal kingdom,
when old and injured, spell out
your wordless book.

What great melancholy
you feel amid the houses
in the village!
How bright

---

11. This probably refers to the eminent French astronomer Camille Flammarion
(1842–1925).

es tu virtud! Aguantas
cuatro carros dormidos,
dos acacias,
y un pozo del antaño
que no tiene agua.

Dando vueltas al mundo,
no encontrarás posada.
No tendrás camposanto
ni mortaja,
ni el aire del amor renovará
tu sustancia.

Pero sal de los campos
y en la negra distancia
de lo eterno, si tallas
la sombra con tu lima
blanca, ¡oh, camino!,
¡pasarás por el puente
de Santa Clara!

El concierto interrumpido

1920

A Adolfo Salazar

Ha roto la armonía
de la noche profunda
el calderón helado y soñoliento
de la media luna.

Las acequias protestan sordamente,
arropadas con juncias,
y las ranas, muecines de la sombra,
se han quedado mudas.

En la vieja taberna del poblado
cesó la triste música,
y ha puesto la sordina a su aristón
la estrella más antigua.

your virtue is! You put up with
four sleeping carts,
two acacias,
and an old-fashioned well
that has no water.

As you circle the world,
you won't find an inn.
You won't have a cemetery
or a shroud,
nor will the air of love rejuvenate
your substance.

But depart from the fields
and in the dark distance
of eternity, if you cut
the shadow with your white
file, O road,
you'll cross the bridge
of Santa Clara![12]

The Interrupted Concert

1920

To Adolfo Salazar

The harmony
of the deep night has been cut short
by the icy, drowsy fermata
of the half-moon.

The irrigation channels protest in muffled tones,
blanketed as they are by rushes,
and the frogs, muezzins of the dark,
have fallen silent.

In the old village tavern
the sad music has stopped,
and the most ancient star
has muted its hurdy-gurdy.

---

12. Probably another reference to the children's song mentioned in footnote 4, page 27.

El viento se ha sentado en los torcales
de la montaña oscura,
y un chopo solitario –el Pitágoras
de la casta llanura–
quiere dar, con su mano centenaria,
un cachete a la luna.

Canción oriental

1920

Es la granada olorosa
un cielo cristalizado.
(Cada grano es una estrella,
cada velo es un ocaso.)
Cielo seco y comprimido
por la garra de los años.
La granada es como un seno
viejo y apergaminado,
cuyo pezón se hizo estrella
para iluminar el campo.

Es colmena diminuta
con panal ensangrentado,
pues con bocas de mujeres
sus abejas la formaron.
Por eso al estallar, ríe
con púrpuras de mil labios . . .

La granada es corazón
que late sobre el sembrado,
un corazón desdeñoso
donde no pican los pájaros,
un corazón que por fuera
es duro como el humano,
pero da al que lo traspasa
olor y sangre de mayo.
La granada es el tesoro
del viejo gnomo del prado,
el que habló con niña Rosa,
en el bosque solitario,
aquél de la blanca barba

The wind has settled in the hollows
of the dark mountain,
and a solitary black-poplar, the Pythagoras
of the chaste plain,
is trying, with its age-old hand,
to slap the moon in the face.

Oriental Song

1920

The fragrant pomegranate
is a crystallized sky.
(Each seed is a star,
each membrane is a sunset.)
A dry sky, compressed
by the talon of the years.

The pomegranate is like a breast
that is old and leathery,
the nipple of which has become a star
to illuminate the countryside.

It is a miniature beehive
with blood-red honeycombs,
since its bees shaped it
out of women's mouths.
Therefore, when it bursts open it laughs
with the purple of a thousand lips.

The pomegranate is a heart
beating upon the sown land,
a scornful heart
where the birds don't peck,
a heart which on the outside
is as hard as a human being's,
but which gives to him who pierces it
the fragrance and blood of May.
The pomegranate is the treasure
of the old gnome in the meadow,
the one who spoke to young Rosa
in the lonely forest,
the one with the white beard

y del traje colorado.
Es el tesoro que aún guardan
las verdes hojas del árbol.
Arca de piedras preciosas
en entraña de oro vago.
La espiga es el pan. Es Cristo
en vida y muerte cuajado.
El olivo es la firmeza
de la fuerza y el trabajo.

La manzana es lo carnal,
fruta esfinge del pecado,
gota de siglos que guarda
de Satanás el contacto.

La naranja es la tristeza
del azahar profanado,
pues se torna fuego y oro
lo que antes fue puro y blanco.

Las vides son la lujuria
que se cuaja en el verano,
de las que la Iglesia saca,
con bendición, licor santo.

Las castañas son la paz
del hogar. Cosas de antaño.
Crepitar de leños viejos,
peregrinos descarriados.

La bellota es la serena
poesía de lo rancio,
y el membrillo de oro débil
la limpieza de lo sano.

Mas la granada es la sangre,
sangre del cielo sagrado,
sangre de la tierra herida
por la aguja del regato.
Sangre del viento que viene
del rudo monte arañado.
Sangre de la mar tranquila,
sangre del dormido lago.
La granada es la prehistoria

and the red costume.
It's the treasure still guarded
by the tree's green leaves.
A coffer of precious stones
in a womb of vague gold.

The grain-ear is bread. It is Christ
made tangible in life and death.

The olive tree is firmness
of strength and labor.

The apple is carnality,
the sphinx-fruit of sin,
an age-old drop that retains
the touch of Satan.

The orange is the sadness
of its profaned blossom,
for that which was formerly pure and white
becomes fiery and golden.

Grapevines are the lustfulness
that solidifies in summer;
from them the Church,
by blessing them, derives a holy beverage.

Chestnuts are the peace
of the fireside. Old-fashioned things.
The crackling of aged firewood,
lost pilgrims.

The acorn is the serene
poetry of good old things,
and the quince, of faint gold,
is the cleanness of good health.

But the pomegranate is blood,
blood of the sacred sky,
blood of the earth wounded
by the needle of the watering ditch.
Blood of the wind which comes
from the rough, scratched mountain.
Blood of the tranquil sea,
blood of the drowsing lake.
The pomegranate is the prehistory

de la sangre que llevamos,
la idea de sangre, encerrada
en glóbulo duro y agrio
que tiene una vaga forma
de corazón y de cráneo.

¡Oh granada abierta!, que eres
una llama sobre el árbol,
hermana en carne de Venus,
risa del huerto oreado.
Te cercan las mariposas,
creyéndote sol parado,
y por miedo de quemarse
huyen de ti los gusanos.

Porque eres luz de la vida,
hembra de las frutas. Claro
lucero de la floresta
del arroyo enamorado.

¡Quién fuera como tú, fruta,
todo pasión sobre el campo!

Chopo muerto

1920

¡Chopo viejo!
Has caído
en el espejo
del remanso dormido,
abatiendo tu frente
ante el poniente.
No fue el vendaval ronco
el que rompió tu tronco,
ni fue el hachazo grave
del leñador, que sabe
has de volver
a nacer.

Fue tu espíritu fuerte
el que llamó a la muerte,
al hallarte sin nidos, olvidado
de los chopos infantes del prado.

of the blood we have inside us,
the Platonic idea of blood, enclosed
in a hard, sour globule
that has the vague shape
of a heart and a cranium.

O open pomegranate! You are
a flame on the tree,
a full sister to Venus,
the laughter of the airy orchard.
The butterflies encircle you,
thinking you're a sun that has stood still,
and for fear of burning up
the worms flee from you.

Because you are the light of life,
the female of the fruits. Bright
evening-star of the grove,
in love with the stream.

If I could only be like you, fruit,
entirely passion in the countryside!

Dead Black-Poplar

1920

Old black-poplar!
You have fallen
into the mirror
of the sleeping pool,
lowering your brow
in the face of the setting sun.
It wasn't the hoarse gale
that broke your trunk,
nor was it the solemn axe-blow
of the woodcutter, who knows
you will be born
again.

It was your strong spirit
which summoned death
when you found yourself without nests, forgotten
by the young poplars in the meadow.

Fue que estabas sediento
de pensamiento,
y tu enorme cabeza, centenaria,
solitaria
escuchaba los lejanos
cantos de tus hermanos.

En tu cuerpo guardabas
las lavas
de tu pasión,
y en tu corazón,
el semen sin futuro de Pegaso.
La terrible simiente
de un amor inocente
por el sol del ocaso.

¡Qué amargura tan honda
para el paisaje:
el héroe de la fronda
sin ramaje!

Ya no serás la cuna
de la luna,
ni la mágica risa
de la brisa,
ni el bastón de un lucero
caballero.
No tornará la primavera
de tu vida,
ni verás la sementera
florecida.
Serás nidal de ranas
y de hormigas.
Tendrás por verdes canas
las ortigas,
y un día la corriente
sonriente
llevará tu corteza
con tristeza.

¡Chopo viejo!
Has caído
en el espejo
del remanso dormido.

It was because you were thirsting
for thought,
and your enormous head, centuries old,
in its loneliness
listened to the distant
songs of your brothers.

   In your body you preserved
the lava
of your passion,
and in your heart
the futureless semen of Pegasus.
The terrible seed
of an innocent love
for the setting sun.

   What deep bitterness
for the landscape:
the hero of foliage
without branches!

   No longer will you be the cradle
of the moon,
nor the magical laughter
of the breeze,
nor the baton of an evening-star
on horseback.
The springtime of your life
will not return,
nor will you see the sown field
blossom.
You'll be the nesting place of frogs
and ants.
For green old-man's hair you'll have
nettles,
and some day the smiling
current
will carry off your bark
sadly.

   Old black-poplar!
You have fallen
into the mirror
of the sleeping pool.

Yo te vi descender
en el atardecer,
y escribo tu elegía,
que es la mía.

Campo

1920

El cielo es de ceniza.
Los árboles son blancos,
y son negros carbones
los rastrojos quemados.
Tiene sangre reseca
la herida del Ocaso,
y el papel incoloro
del monte está arrugado.
El polvo del camino
se esconde en los barrancos.
Están las fuentes turbias
y quietos los remansos.
Suena en un gris rojizo
la esquila del rebaño,
y la noria materna
acabó su rosario.

El cielo es de ceniza.
Los árboles son blancos.

La balada del agua del mar

1920

A Emilio Prados (cazador de nubes)

El mar
sonríe a lo lejos.
Dientes de espuma,
labios de cielo.

—¿Qué vendes, oh joven turbia,
con los senos al aire?

I saw you descend
as evening fell,
and I'm writing your elegy,
which is also mine.

Countryside

1920

The sky is ashen.
The trees are white,
and the burnt stubble
is black coal.
The wound in the west
has dried blood on it,
and the colorless paper
of the mountain is creased.
The dust from the road
hides in the gullies.
The fountains are muddied
and the pools still.
The bells of the flock
resound in a reddish gray,
and the maternal waterwheel
has completed its rosary.

The sky is ashen.
The trees are white.

The Ballad of the Water of the Sea

1920

To Emilio Prados (cloud-hunter)

The sea
smiles far off.
Teeth of foam,
lips of sky.

"What are you selling, O troubled young woman,
with your firm, high breasts?"

–Vendo, señor, el agua
de los mares.
–¿Qué llevas, oh negro joven,
mezclado con tu sangre?
–Llevo, señor, el agua
de los mares.
–¿Esas lágrimas salobres
de dónde vienen, madre?
–Lloro, señor, el agua
de los mares.
–Corazón, ¿y esta amargura
seria, de dónde nace?
–¡Amarga mucho el agua
de los mares!

El mar
sonríe a lo lejos.
Dientes de espuma,
labios de cielo.

Árboles

1919

¡Árboles!
¿Habéis sido flechas
caídas del azul?
¿Qué terribles guerreros os lanzaron?
¿Han sido las estrellas?

Vuestras músicas vienen del alma de los pájaros,
de los ojos de Dios,
de la pasión perfecta.
¡Árboles!
¿Conocerán vuestras raíces toscas
mi corazón en tierra?

"Sir, I'm selling the water
of the seas."

What do you have, O dark young man,
mingled with your blood?"

"Sir, I have the water
of the seas."

"Those brackish tears,
where do they come from, old lady?"

"Sir, I'm weeping the water
of the seas."

"My heart: this deep
bitterness, where does it spring from?"

"Very bitter, the water
of the seas!"

The sea
smiles far-off.
Teeth of foam,
lips of sky.

Trees

1919

Trees!
Were you once arrows
fallen from the blue?
What fearsome warriors shot you?
Was it the stars?

Your music comes from the soul of the birds,
from the eyes of God,
from perfect passion.
Trees!
Will your rough roots recognize
my heart in the earth?

La luna y la Muerte

1919

La luna tiene dientes de marfil.
¡Qué vieja y triste asoma!
Están los cauces secos,
los campos sin verdores
y los árboles mustios
sin nidos y sin hojas.
Doña Muerte, arrugada,
pasea por sauzales
con su absurdo cortejo
de ilusiones remotas.
Va vendiendo colores
de cera y de tormenta
como un hada de cuento
mala y enredadora.
La luna le ha comprado
pinturas a la Muerte.
En esta noche turbia
¡está la luna loca!
Yo mientras tanto pongo
en mi pecho sombrío
una feria sin músicas
con las tiendas de sombra.

Madrigal

1919

Yo te miré a los ojos
cuando era niño y bueno.
Tus manos me rozaron
y me distes un beso.

(Los relojes llevan la misma cadencia,
y las noches tienen las mismas estrellas.)

The Moon and Death

1919

The moon has ivory teeth.
How old and sad it looks as it comes into view!
The watercourses are dry,
the fields devoid of green,
and the trees withered,
without nests or leaves.
Lady Death, wrinkled,
proceeds through stands of willow
with her absurd retinue
of remote hopes.
She is selling paints
made of wax and tempest
like a fairy in a folktale,
a wicked troublemaker.

The moon has purchased
paints from Death.
On this hazy night
the moon is a madwoman!

Meanwhile I place
in my somber bosom
a fair without musicians
with tents of shadow.

Madrigal

1919

I looked into your eyes
when I was a child, and good.
Your hands grazed me
and you gave[13] me a kiss.

(The clocks keep the same cadence,
and the nights have the same stars.)

---

13. The authenticity here of the colloquial form *distes* (instead of *diste*) is guaranteed by the syllable count.

Y se abrió mi corazón
como una flor bajo el cielo,
los pétalos de lujuria
y los estambres de sueño.

(Los relojes llevan la misma cadencia,
y las noches tienen las mismas estrellas.)

En mi cuarto sollozaba
como el príncipe del cuento
por Estrellita de Oro
que se fue de los torneos.

(Los relojes llevan la misma cadencia,
y las noches tienen las mismas estrellas.)

Yo me alejé de tu lado
queriéndote sin saberlo.
No sé cómo son tus ojos,
tus manos ni tus cabellos.
Sólo me queda en la frente
la mariposa del beso.

(Los relojes llevan la misma cadencia,
y las noches tienen las mismas estrellas.)

Deseo

1920

Sólo tu corazón caliente,
y nada más.

Mi paraíso un campo
sin ruiseñor
ni liras,
con un río discreto
y una fuentecilla.

Sin la espuela del viento
sobre la fronda,
ni la estrella que quiere
ser hoja.

Una enorme luz
que fuera

And my heart opened
like a flower under the sky,
its petals made of lust
and its stamens of dream.

(The clocks keep the same cadence,
and the nights have the same stars.)

In my room, I'd sob
like the prince in the fairy tale
for Little Golden Star,
who departed from the tournament.

(The clocks keep the same cadence,
and the nights have the same stars.)

I left you,
in love with you without knowing it.
I don't know what your eyes are like,
or your hands and hair.
All that remains on my brow
is the butterfly of the kiss.

(The clocks keep the same cadence,
and the nights have the same stars.)

Desire

1920

Only your hot heart,
and nothing else.

My paradise a countryside
without nightingale
or lyres,
with a discreet river
and a little fountain.

Without the wind's spur
over the foliage,
or the star that wants
to be a leaf.

A vast light
that could be

luciérnaga
de otra,
en un campo de
miradas rotas.

Un reposo claro
y allí nuestros besos,
lunares sonoros
del eco,
se abrirían muy lejos.

Y tu corazón caliente,
nada más.

Los álamos de plata

Mayo de 1919

Los álamos de plata
se inclinan sobre el agua.
Ellos todo lo saben pero nunca hablarán.
El lirio de la fuente
no grita su tristeza.
¡Todo es más digno que la humanidad!

La ciencia del silencio frente al cielo estrellado,
la posee la flor y el insecto no más.
La ciencia de los cantos por los cantos la tienen
los bosques rumorosos
y las aguas del mar.

El silencio profundo de la vida en la tierra,
nos lo enseña la rosa
abierta en el rosal.

¡Hay que dar el perfume
que encierran nuestras almas!
Hay que ser todo cantos,
todo luz y bondad.
¡Hay que abrirse del todo
frente a la noche negra,
para que nos llenemos de rocío inmortal!

!Hay que acostar al cuerpo
dentro del alma inquieta!

the firefly
of another light,
in a countryside of
broken glances.

A bright resting place
and, there, our kisses,
resounding birthmarks
of the echo,
would open out to a great distance.

And your hot heart,
nothing else.

The Silver Poplars

May 1919

The silver poplars
stoop over the water.
They know everything but will never speak.
The iris of the fountain
doesn't cry out its sadness.
Everything is more dignified than mankind!

The silence's knowledge when faced by the starry sky
is possessed by flowers and insects alone.
The knowledge of song for song's sake is possessed by
the rustling forests
and the waters of the sea.

The deep silence of life on earth
is taught to us by the rose
unfurled on the rosebush.

We must bestow the fragrance
that our souls enclose!
We must be completely song,
completely light and goodness.
We must open ourselves entirely
to the black night,
to fill ourselves with immortal dew!

We must lay our body down
inside our restless soul!

Hay que cegar los ojos con luz de más allá.
Tenemos que asomarnos
a la sombra del pecho,
y arrancar las estrellas que nos puso Satán.

Hay que ser como el árbol
que siempre está rezando,
como el agua del cauce
fija en la eternidad.

¡Hay que arañarse el alma con garras de tristeza
para que entren las llamas
del horizonte astral!

Brotaría en la sombra del amor carcomido
una fuente de aurora
tranquila y maternal.
Desaparecerían ciudades en el viento
y a Dios en una nube
veríamos pasar.

Espigas

Junio de 1919

El trigal se ha entregado a la muerte.
Ya las hoces cortan las espigas.
Cabecean los chopos hablando
con el alma sutil de la brisa.

El trigal sólo quiere silencio.
Se cuajó con el sol, y suspira
por el amplio elemento en que moran
los ensueños dispertos.
                    El día,
ya maduro de luz y sonido,
por los montes azules declina.

¿Qué misterioso pensamiento
conmueve a las espigas?
¿Qué ritmo de tristeza soñadora
los trigales agita? . . .

¡Parecen las espigas viejos pájaros
que no pueden volar!

We must blind our eyes with light from beyond.
We have to show our face
in the shadow of our bosom,
and tear out the stars that Satan planted in us.

We must be like the tree,
which is always praying,
like the water in the channel,
attentive to eternity.

We must scratch our soul with claws of sadness
so that the flames of the astral
horizon may enter!

In the shadow of worm-eaten love there would well up
a fountain of dawn,
tranquil and maternal.
Cities would vanish in the wind
and we'd see God
passing by on a cloud.

Ears of Grain

June 1919

The wheatfield has surrendered to death.
The sickles are already cutting the ears.
The black-poplars nod, speaking
with the subtle soul of the breeze.

The wheatfield asks only for silence.
It filled itself in the sun, and it sighs
for the ample element in which
waking dreams dwell.
                        The day,
now ripe with light and sound,
is declining on the blue mountains.

What mysterious thoughts
agitate the grain?
What rhythm of dreamy sadness
stirs the wheatfields? . . .

The ears of grain resemble old birds
that can't fly!

Son cabecitas,
que tienen el cerebro de oro puro
y expresiones tranquilas.
Todas piensan lo mismo,
                    todas llevan
un secreto profundo que meditan.
Arrancan a la tierra su oro vivo
y, cual dulces abejas del sol, liban
el rayo abrasador con que se visten
para formar el alma de la harina.

   ¡Oh, qué alegre tristeza me causáis,
dulcísimas espigas!
Venís de las edades más profundas,
cantasteis en la Biblia,
y tocáis cuando os rozan los silencios
un concierto de liras.

   Brotáis para alimento de los hombres,
¡pero mirad las blancas margaritas
y los lirios que nacen *porque sí!*
¡Momias de oro sobre las campiñas!
La flor silvestre nace para el Sueño
y vosotras nacéis para la vida.

Meditación bajo la lluvia

Fragmento

3 de enero de 1919

A José Mora

   Ha besado la lluvia al jardín provinciano
dejando emocionantes cadencias en las hojas.
El aroma sereno de la tierra mojada
inunda al corazón de tristeza remota.

   Se rasgan nubes grises en el mudo horizonte.
Sobre el agua dormida de la fuente, las gotas
se clavan, levantando claras perlas de espuma.
Fuegos fatuos que apaga el temblor de las ondas.

   La pena de la tarde estremece a mi pena.
Se ha llenado el jardín de ternura monótona.

They're little heads
with a brain of pure gold
and calm expressions.

They all have the same thought,
                              they all have
a deep secret on which they ponder.
They tear out the earth's living gold
and, like sweet bees of the sun, they sip
the scorching beam in which they dress
to form the soul of the flour.

Oh, what joyful sadness you give me,
you very sweet ears of grain!
You come from the remotest epochs,
you sang in the Bible,
and when silence brushes against you, you play
a consort of lyres.

You germinate for the sustenance of man.
But look at the white daisies
and the irises, which are born "just because"!
Golden mummies in the fields!
The woodland flower is born for Sleep
and you are born to be life.

Meditation in the Rain

A Fragment

January 3, 1919

To José Mora

The rain has kissed the provincial garden,
leaving stirring cadences on the leaves.
The serene fragrance of the moist earth
floods the heart with distant sadness.

Gray clouds are ripped open on the mute horizon.
On the sleeping water of the fountain, the raindrops
dig in, casting up bright pearls of foam.
Will-o'-the-wisps extinguished by the trembling of the waves.

The sorrow of the afternoon stirs up my own.
The garden has become filled with monotonous tenderness.

¿Todo mi sufrimiento se ha de perder, Dios mío,
como se pierde el dulce sonido de las frondas?

¿Todo el eco de estrellas que guardo sobre el alma
será luz que me ayude a luchar con mi forma?
¿Y el alma verdadera se despierta en la muerte?
¿Y esto que ahora pensamos se lo traga la sombra?

¡Oh, qué tranquilidad del jardín con la lluvia!
Todo el paisaje casto mi corazón transforma,
en un ruido de ideas humildes y apenadas
que pone en mis entrañas un batir de palomas.
    Sale el sol.
              El jardín desangra en amarillo.
Late sobre el ambiente una pena que ahoga.
Yo siento la nostalgia de mi infancia intranquila,
mi ilusión de ser grande en el amor, las horas
pasadas como ésta contemplando la lluvia
con tristeza nativa.
                 Caperucita roja
iba por el sendero . . .
Se fueron mis historias, hoy medito, confuso,
ante la fuente turbia que del amor me brota.

¿Todo mi sufrimiento se ha de perder, Dios mío,
como se pierde el dulce sonido de las frondas?

    Vuelve a llover.
El viento va trayendo a las sombras.

Manantial

Fragmento

1919

La sombra se ha dormido en la pradera.
Los manantiales cantan.

Frente al ancho crepúsculo de invierno
mi corazón soñaba.
¿Quién pudiera entender los manantiales,
el secreto del agua
recién nacida, ese cantar oculto

Will all my suffering die away, O God,
as the soft sound of the leaves dies away?

Will all the echo of stars that I keep in my soul
be light to help me struggle with my form?
And does the true soul awaken at death?
And are our present thoughts swallowed up by shadow?

Oh, how calm the garden is in the rain!
My heart transforms the whole chaste landscape
into a sound of humble, grieving ideas
which sets doves' wings beating inside me.

The sun comes out.
                    The garden loses yellow blood.
A stifling sorrow throbs upon the surroundings.
I feel a nostalgia for my restless childhood,
my hopes of being great in love, the hours
spent, like this one, contemplating the rain
with inborn sadness.
                    Little Red Riding Hood
was walking down the path . . .
My stories are gone; today I meditate in confusion,
confronting the clouded fountain that wells up from my love.

Will all my suffering die away, O God,
as the soft sound of the leaves dies away?

It's raining again.
The wind is bringing the shadows.

Fountain

A Fragment

1919

The shadow has fallen asleep in the meadow.
The fountains sing.

In the face of the broad winter twilight
my heart was dreaming.
If I could only understand the fountains,
the secret of the newborn
water, that song hidden

a todas las miradas
del espíritu, dulce melodía
más allá de las almas? . . .

   Luchando bajo el peso de la sombra
un manantial cantaba.
Yo me acerqué para escuchar su canto
pero mi corazón no entiende nada.

   Era un brotar de estrellas invisibles
sobre la hierba casta,
nacimiento del Verbo de la tierra
por un sexo sin mancha.

   Mi chopo centenario de la vega
sus hojas meneaba
y eran las hojas trémulas de ocaso
como estrellas de plata.
El resumen de un cielo de verano
era el gran chopo.
                        Mansas
y turbias de penumbra yo sentía
las canciones del agua.

   ¿Qué alfabeto de auroras ha compuesto
sus ocultas palabras?
¿Qué labios las pronuncian? ¿Y qué dicen
a la estrella lejana?
¡Mi corazón es malo, Señor! Siento en mi carne
la inaplacable brasa
del pecado. Mis mares interiores
se quedaron sin playas.
Tu faro se apagó. ¡Ya los alumbra
mi corazón de llamas!
Pero el negro secreto de la noche
y el secreto del agua
¿son misterios tan sólo para el ojo
de la conciencia humana?
¿La niebla del misterio no estremece
al árbol, el insecto y la montaña?
¿El terror de la sombra no lo sienten
las piedras y las plantas?
¿Es sonido tan sólo esta voz mía?
¿Y el casto manantial no dice nada?

from every gaze
of the mind, a sweet melody
beyond all souls! . . .

Struggling beneath the weight of shadow,
a fountain was singing.
I drew nearer to listen to its song
but my heart doesn't understand a thing.

It was a welling-up of invisible stars
onto the chaste grass,
the birth of the Word of earth
from immaculate genitals.

My age-old black-poplar of the plain
was waving its leaves
and those leaves were tremulous with sunset
like silver stars.
The great poplar was the summary
of a summer sky.
                    Gentle
and clouded with penumbra were the songs
of the water that I heard.

What alphabet of dawns comprised
its occult words?
What lips pronounce them? And what do they say
to the distant star?
My heart is sick, Lord! I feel in my flesh
the unappeasable blaze
of sin. My inner seas
have been left beachless.
Your beacon has gone out. They are now lighted
by my flaming heart!
But the night's black secret
and the water's secret:
are they mysteries only to the eye
of human consciousness?
Doesn't the fog of mystery stir up
the tree, the insect, and the mountain?
Isn't the terror of the shadow felt by
the stones and plants?
Is this voice of mine mere sound?
And does the chaste fountain say nothing?

Mas yo siento en el agua
algo que me estremece . . . como un aire
que agita los ramajes de mi alma.
«¡Sé árbol!»
          (dijo una voz en la distancia).
Y hubo un torrente de luceros
sobre el cielo sin mancha.

Yo me incrusté en el chopo centenario
con tristeza y con ansia,
cual Dafne varonil que huye miedosa
de un Apolo de sombra y de nostalgia.
Mi espíritu fundióse con las hojas
y fue mi sangre savia.
En untosa resina convirtióse
la fuente de mis lágrimas.
El corazón se fue con las raíces,
y mi pasión humana,
haciendo heridas en la ruda carne,
fugaz me abandonaba.

Frente al ancho crepúsculo de invierno
yo torcía las ramas
gozando de los ritmos ignorados
entre la brisa helada.
Sentí sobre mis brazos dulces nidos,
acariciar de alas,
y sentí mil abejas campesinas
que en mis dedos zumbaban.
¡Tenía una colmena de oro vivo
en las viejas entrañas!
El paisaje y la tierra se perdieron,
sólo el cielo quedaba,
y escuché el débil ruido de los astros
y el respirar de las montañas.

¿No podrán comprender mis dulces hojas
el secreto del agua?
¿Llegarán mis raíces a los reinos
donde nace y se cuaja?
Incliné mis ramajes hacia el cielo
que las ondas copiaban,
mojé las hojas en el cristalino

But I feel in the water
something that stirs me . . . like a gust
shaking my soul's branches.

"Be a tree!"
                    (said a voice in the distance).
And there was a torrent of bright stars
in the spotless sky.

I embedded myself in the age-old poplar
sadly and anxiously,
like a male Daphne fleeing in fear
from an Apollo of shadow and nostalgia.
My spirit merged with the leaves
and my blood became sap.
The fountain of my tears
was converted to oily resin.
My heart departed to the roots,
and my human passion,
making wounds in the rough flesh,
was deserting me in great haste.

In the face of the broad winter twilight
I was twisting my boughs,
enjoying the unfamiliar rhythms
in the icy breeze.
On my arms I felt soft nests,
the caress of wings,
and I felt a thousand wild bees
buzzing on my fingers.
I had a hive of living gold
in my ancient interior!
The landscape and the earth were lost to me,
only the sky remained,
and I listened to the faint sound of the planets
and the breathing of the mountains.

Won't my gentle leaves be able to comprehend
the water's secret?
Will my roots reach the realms
where it is born and comes together?
I bent my branches toward the sky
as it was copied in the waves,
I wet my leaves in the crystalline

diamante azul que canta,
y sentí borbotar los manantiales
como de humano yo los escuchara.
Era el mismo fluir lleno de música
y de ciencia ignorada.

   Al levantar mis brazos gigantescos
frente al azul, estaba
lleno de niebla espesa, de rocío
y de luz marchitada.

   Tuve la gran tristeza vegetal,
el amor a las alas,
para poder lanzarse con los vientos
a las estrellas blancas.
Pero mi corazón en las raíces
triste me murmuraba:
«Si no comprendes a los manantiales,
¡muere y troncha tus ramas!»

   ¡Señor, arráncame del suelo! ¡Dame oídos
que entiendan a las aguas!
Dame una voz que por amor arranque
su secreto a las ondas encantadas;
para encender tu faro sólo pido
aceite de palabras.

   «¡Sé ruiseñor!», dice una voz perdida
en la muerta distancia.
Y un torrente de cálidos luceros
brotó del seno que la noche guarda.
. . . .
. . . .

Mar

Abril de 1919

   El mar es
el Lucifer del azul.
El cielo caído
por querer ser la luz.

   ¡Pobre mar condenado

blue singing diamond,
and I heard the fountains bubble
as when I had heard them in my human state.
It was the same flowing, filled with music
and unfamiliar knowledge.

When I raised my gigantic arms
to face the blue, it was
filled with thick mist, dew,
and faded light.

I felt the great sadness of plants,
love in my wings,
so I could fling myself, with the winds,
at the white stars.
But at my roots my heart
murmured to me sadly:
"If you don't understand the fountains,
die and break your boughs!"

Lord, rip me out of the ground! Give me ears
that can understand the waters!
Give me a voice that, through love, can tear
the enchanted waves' secret from them;
to light your beacon, all I ask is
the oil of words.

"Be a nightingale!" says a voice lost
in the dead distance.
And a torrent of hot bright stars
gushed from the breast that the night protects.

. . . .
. . . .

Sea

April 1919

The sea is
the Lucifer of the blue.
The sky fallen
because it wanted to be the light.

Poor sea, condemned

a eterno movimiento,
habiendo antes estado
quieto en el firmamento!

Pero de tu amargura
te redimió el amor.
Pariste a Venus pura,
y quedóse tu hondura
virgen y sin dolor.

Tus tristezas son bellas,
mar de espasmos gloriosos.
Mas hoy en vez de estrellas
tienes pulpos verdosos.

Aguanta tu sufrir,
formidable Satán.
Cristo anduvo por ti,
mas también lo hizo Pan.

La estrella Venus es
la armonía del mundo.
¡Calle el Eclesiastés!
Venus es lo profundo
del alma . . .

. . . Y el hombre miserable
es un ángel caído.
La tierra es el probable
paraíso perdido.

Sueño

Mayo de 1919

Iba yo montado sobre
un macho cabrío.
El abuelo me habló
y me dijo:
«Ése es tu camino.»
«¡Es ése!», gritó mi sombra,
disfrazada de mendigo.
«¡Es aquel de oro!», dijeron
mis vestidos.

to eternal movement,
though formerly you were
stationary in the firmament!

But from your bitterness
you were redeemed by love.
You gave birth to pure Venus,
and your depths remained
virginal, not feeling pain.

Your sad moods are beautiful,
sea of glorious spasms.
But today in place of stars
you have greenish octopuses.

Endure your suffering,
formidable Satan.
Christ walked on you,
but so did Pan.

The star Venus is
the harmony of the world.
Let Ecclesiastes be silent!
Venus is the depths
of the soul . . .

. . . And wretched man
is a fallen angel.
The earth is probably
our lost paradise.

Dream

May 1919

I was riding on
a he-goat.
The old fellow spoke to me,
saying:
"This is your path."
"It's that one!" shouted my shadow,
disguised as a beggar.
"It's that golden one farther off!" said
my clothes.

Un gran cisne me guiñó,
diciendo: «¡Vente conmigo!»
Y una serpiente mordía
mi sayal de peregrino.

Mirando al cielo, pensaba:
«Yo no tengo camino.
Las rosas del fin serán
como las del principio.
En niebla se convierte
la carne y el rocío.»

Mi caballo fantástico me lleva
por un campo rojizo.
«¡Déjame!», clamó, llorando,
mi corazón pensativo.
Yo lo abandoné en la tierra,
lleno de tristeza.
                    Vino
la noche, llena de arrugas
y de sombras.

           Alumbran el camino,
los ojos luminosos y azulados
de mi macho cabrío.

Encina

1919

Bajo tu casta sombra, encina vieja,
quiero sondar la fuente de mi vida
y sacar de los fangos de mi sombra
las esmeraldas líricas.

Echo mis redes sobre el agua turbia
y las saco vacías.
¡Más abajo del cieno tenebroso
están mis pedrerías!

¡Hunde en mi pecho tus ramajes santos,
oh solitaria encina,
y deja en mi sub-alma
tus secretos y tu pasión tranquila!

A big swan winked at me,
saying: "Come with me!"
And a snake was biting
my pilgrim-style sackcloth.

Looking at the sky, I thought:
"I have no path.
The roses at the end will be
like those at the beginning.
Flesh and dew
become mist."

My fantasy-horse is taking me
across a reddish field.
"Leave me behind!" my pensive heart
exclaimed tearfully.
I abandoned it on the ground,
filled with sadness.
⠀⠀⠀⠀⠀⠀⠀Night
came, full of wrinkles
and shadows.

⠀⠀⠀⠀⠀The path is illuminated
by the luminous, bluish eyes
of my he-goat.

Holm Oak

1919

In your chaste shade, old holm oak,
I wish to plumb the fountain of my life
and to draw from the mire of my shadow
the lyrical emeralds.

I cast my nets onto the muddied water
and pull them out empty.
My precious stones are
lower down than the shadowy mud!

Sink your holy branches into my breast,
O solitary oak,
and leave behind in my sub-soul
your secrets and your tranquil passion!

Esta tristeza juvenil se pasa,
¡ya lo sé! La alegría
otra vez dejará sus guirnaldas
sobre mi frente herida,
aunque nunca mis redes pescarán
la oculta pedrería
de tristeza inconsciente que reluce
al fondo de mi vida.

Pero mi gran dolor trascendental
es tu dolor, encina.
Es el mismo dolor de las estrellas
y de la flor marchita.

Mis lágrimas resbalan a la tierra
y, como tus resinas,
corren sobre las aguas del gran cauce
que va a la noche fría.
Y nosotros también resbalaremos,
yo con mis pedrerías,
y tú plenas las ramas de invisibles
bellotas metafísicas.

No me abandones nunca en mis pesares,
esquelética amiga.
Cántame con tu boca vieja y casta
una canción antigua,
con palabras de tierra entrelazadas
en la azul melodía.

Vuelvo otra vez a echar las redes sobre
la fuente de mi vida,
redes hechas con hilos de esperanza,
nudos de poesía,
y saco piedras falsas entre un cieno
de pasiones dormidas.

Con el sol del otoño toda el agua
de mi fontana vibra,
y noto que sacando sus raíces
huye de mí la encina.

This youthful sadness will pass,
I know! Joy
will once more leave its garlands
on my wounded brow,
though my nets will never fish up
the hidden jewels
of unconscious sadness that shine
in the depths of my life.

But my great transcendental sorrow
is also yours, oak.
It is the same sorrow shared by the stars
and the faded flower.

My tears trickle to the earth
and, like your resin,
flow into the waters of the great channel
that is heading for the cold night.
And we, too, shall trickle away,
I with my jewels,
and you with your boughs full of invisible
metaphysical acorns.

Never abandon me in my troubles,
skeletal friend.
Sing to me with your old, chaste lips
an ancient song,
with earthen words interlaced
in the blue melody.

Once again I cast my nets onto
the fountain of my life,
nets woven with cords of hope,
knots of poetry,
and I draw up false stones from a mire
of sleeping passions.

With the autumn sun all the water
of my fountain vibrates,
and I observe that the oak pulls up its roots
and flees from me.

Invocación al laurel

1919

A *Pepe Cienfuegos*

   Por el horizonte confuso y doliente
venía la noche preñada de estrellas.
Yo, como el barbudo mago de los cuentos,
sabía lenguajes de flores y piedras.

   Aprendí secretos de melancolía,
dichos por cipreses, ortigas y yedras;
supe del ensueño por boca del nardo,
canté con los lirios canciones serenas.

   En el bosque antiguo, lleno de negrura,
todos me mostraban sus almas cual eran:
el pinar, borracho de aroma y sonido;
los olivos viejos, cargados de ciencia;
los álamos muertos, nidales de hormigas;
el musgo, nevado de blancas violetas.

   Todo hablaba dulce a mi corazón
temblando en los hilos de sonora seda
con que el agua envuelve las cosas paradas
como telaraña de armonía eterna.

   Las rosas estaban soñando en la lira,
tejen las encinas oros de leyendas,
y entre la tristeza viril de los robles
dicen los enebros temores de aldea.

   Yo comprendo toda la pasión del bosque:
ritmo de la hoja, ritmo de la estrella.
Mas decidme, ¡oh cedros!, si mi corazón
dormirá en los brazos de la luz perfecta.

   Conozco la lira que presientes, rosa;
formé su cordaje con mi vida muerta.
¡Dime en qué remanso podré abandonarla
como se abandonan las pasiones viejas!

   ¡Conozco el misterio que cantas, ciprés;
soy hermano tuyo en noche y en pena;

Invocation to the Laurel

1919

To Pepe Cienfuegos

Over the confused, aching horizon
night was coming, pregnant with stars.
I, like the long-bearded wizard in fairy tales,
knew the languages of flowers and stones.

I learned secrets of melancholy,
told by cypresses, nettles, and ivies;
I heard about the dream from the lips of the amaryllis,
with the irises I sang calm songs.

In the ancient forest, full of blackness,
they would all show me their true souls:
the pinewood, drunk on fragrance and sound;
the old olive trees, laden with knowledge;
the dead poplars, nesting places for ants;
the moss, snowy with white violets.

Everything would speak softly to my heart
as it trembled on the threads of rustling silk
with which water envelops stationary things
like a spiderweb of eternal harmony.

The roses were dreaming on the lyre,
the holm oaks weave the gold of legends,
and amid the virile sadness of the oaks
the junipers told of village fears.

I understand all the passion of the forest:
rhythm of the leaf, rhythm of the star.
But tell me, cedars, whether my heart
will sleep in the arms of perfect light.

I know the lyre that you foresee, rose;
I fashioned its strings from my dead life.
Tell me in what pool I can abandon it,
the way that old passions are left behind!

I know the mystery that you sing, cypress;
I am your brother in night and sorrow;

tenemos la entraña cuajada de nidos,
tú de ruiseñores y yo de tristezas!

¡Conozco tu encanto sin fin, padre olivo,
al darnos la sangre que extraes de la Tierra:
como tú, yo extraigo con mi sentimiento
el óleo bendito
que tiene la idea!

Todos me abrumáis con vuestras canciones;
yo sólo os pregunto por la mía incierta;
ninguno queréis sofocar las ansias
de este fuego casto
que el pecho me quema.

¡Oh laurel divino, de alma inaccesible,
siempre silencioso,
lleno de nobleza!
¡Vierte en mis oídos tu historia divina,
tu sabiduría profunda y sincera!

¡Árbol que produces frutos de silencio,
maestro de besos y mago de orquestas,
formado del cuerpo rosado de Dafne
con savia potente de Apolo en tus venas!

¡Oh gran sacerdote del saber antiguo!
¡Oh mudo solemne cerrado a las quejas!
¡Todos tus hermanos del bosque me hablan;
sólo tú, severo, mi canción desprecias!

Acaso, ¡oh maestro del ritmo!, medites
lo inútil del triste llorar del poeta.
Acaso tus hojas, manchadas de luna,
pierdan la ilusión de la primavera.

La dulzura tenue del anochecer,
cual negro rocío, tapizó la senda,
teniendo de inmenso dosel a la noche,
que venía grave, preñada de estrellas.

our insides are filled with nests,
yours with nightingales, mine with sadness!

I know your limitless delight, father olive tree,
in giving us the blood you extract from the Earth:
like you, with my feelings I extract
the holy oil
contained in the idea!

You all overwhelm me with your songs;
I only ask you about my own uncertain one;
not one of you wishes to smother the anxiety
of this chaste fire
which is burning my breast.

O divine laurel with the unreachable soul,
you that are always silent,
full of nobility!
Pour into my ears your divine story,
your profound, sincere wisdom!

You tree that produce fruits of silence,
teacher of kisses and wizard of orchestras,
fashioned from Daphne's pink body
with the potent sap of Apollo in your veins!

O high priest of ancient knowledge!
O solemn mute, impervious to laments!
All your brothers of the forest speak to me;
only you severely scorn my song!

Perhaps, O teacher of rhythm, you are meditating
on the pointlessness of the poet's sad weeping.
Perhaps your leaves, flecked with moonlight,
are losing the hopes they held in springtime.

The delicate softness of the nightfall,
like black dew, carpeted the path,
having the night as an immense canopy,
the night which came solemnly, pregnant with stars.

Ritmo de otoño

1920

A *Manuel Ángeles*

Amargura dorada en el paisaje.
El corazón escucha.
En la tristeza húmeda
el viento dijo:
«Yo soy todo de estrellas derretidas,
sangre del infinito.
Con mi roce descubro los colores
de los fondos dormidos.
Voy herido de místicas miradas,
yo llevo los suspiros
en burbujas de sangre invisibles
hacia el sereno triunfo
del Amor inmortal lleno de Noche.
Me conocen los niños,
y me cuajo en tristezas
sobre cuentos de reinas y castillos.
Soy copa de la luz. Soy incensario
de cantos desprendidos
que cayeron envueltos en azules
transparencias de ritmo.
En mi alma perdiéronse solemnes
carne y alma de Cristo,
y finjo la tristeza de la tarde
melancólico y frío.
Soy la eterna armonía de la Tierra,
el bosque innumerable.

Llevo las carabelas de los sueños
a lo desconocido
Y tengo la amargura solitaria
de no saber mi fin ni mi destino.»

Las palabras del viento eran suaves,
con hondura de lirios.
Mi corazón durmióse en la tristeza
del crepúsculo.

Sobre la parda tierra de la estepa

Autumnal Rhythm

1920

To Manuel Ángeles

Gilded bitterness in the landscape.
The heart listens.

In the damp sadness
the wind said:
"I am entirely made up of melted stars,
the blood of infinity.
As I brush by, I reveal the colors
of the sleeping depths.
I am wounded by mystic gazes,
I carry sighs
in invisible bubbles of blood
to the serene triumph
of immortal Love full of Night.
The children know me,
and I congeal into sadness
when they hear tales of queens and castles.
I am a goblet of light. I am a censer
of detached songs
that fell, enveloped in blue
transparencies of rhythm.
In my soul were solemnly lost
the flesh and soul of Christ,
and I mimic the evening's sadness
with my cold melancholy.
I am the eternal harmony of Earth,
the uncountable woods.

"I carry the caravels of dreams
into the unknown.
And I have the lonely bitterness
of not knowing my end or my destiny."

The wind's words were gentle,
with the profundity of irises.
My heart fell asleep in the sadness
of dusk.

On the brown soil of the steppe

los gusanos dijeron sus delirios:
«Soportamos tristezas
al borde del camino.
Sabemos de las flores de los bosques,
del canto monocorde de los grillos,
de la lira sin cuerdas que pulsamos,
del oculto sendero que seguimos.
Nuestro ideal no llega a las estrellas,
es sereno, sencillo;
quisiéramos hacer miel, como abejas,
o tener dulce voz o fuerte grito,
o fácil caminar sobre las hierbas,
o senos donde mamen nuestros hijos.
    Dichosos los que nacen mariposas
o tienen luz de luna en su vestido.
¡Dichosos los que cortan la rosa
y recogen el trigo!
¡Dichosos los que dudan de la Muerte
teniendo Paraíso,
y el aire que recorre lo que quiere
seguro de infinito!
Dichosos los gloriosos y los fuertes,
los que jamás fueron compadecidos,
los que bendijo y sonrió triunfante
el hermano Francisco.
Pasamos mucha pena
cruzando los caminos.
Quisiéramos saber lo que nos hablan
los álamos del río.»

    Y en la muda tristeza de la tarde
respondióles el polvo del camino:
«Dichosos, ¡oh gusanos!, que tenéis
justa conciencia de vosotros mismos,
y formas y pasiones
y hogares encendidos.
Yo en el sol me disuelvo
siguiendo al peregrino,
y cuando pienso ya en la luz quedarme
caigo al suelo dormido.»

    Los gusanos lloraron y los árboles,

the worms told their deliriums:
"We endure sadness
at the side of the road.
We learn from the flowers in the forest,
from the monotone call of the crickets,
from the stringless lyre that we strum,
from the hidden path that we follow.
Our ideal doesn't reach the stars,
it's calm and simple;
we'd like to make honey, like bees,
or have a sweet voice or a loud cry,
or to have an easy journey through the grass,
or breasts at which our children could suckle.

    "Lucky are they who are born as butterflies
or have moonlight on their garment.
Lucky are they who cut the rose
and gather the wheat!
Lucky are they who are in doubt about Death,
possessing Paradise,
and the breeze that travels wherever it wishes,
certain of infinity!
Lucky are those glorious and strong ones,
those who never were pitied,
those blessed, as he smiled triumphantly,
by Brother Francis.
We endure much grief
when crossing roads.
We'd like to know that which is told us
by the poplars at the river."

    And in the mute sadness of the evening
the dust of the road replied to them:
"You are lucky, worms, because you possess
a true awareness of yourselves,
and forms and passions
and lighted hearths.
Whereas I dissolve in the sunshine
as I follow the pilgrim,
and when I think I shall now remain in the light,
I fall onto the sleeping soil."

    The worms wept, and the trees,

moviendo sus cabezas pensativos,
dijeron: «El azul es imposible.
Creímos alcanzarlo cuando niños,
y quisiéramos ser como las águilas
ahora que estamos por el rayo heridos.
De las águilas es todo el azul.»
Y el águila a lo lejos:
«¡No, no es mío!
Porque el azul lo tienen las estrellas
entre sus claros brillos.»
Las estrellas: «Tampoco lo tenemos:
está sobre nosotras escondido.»
Y la negra distancia: «El azul
lo tiene la esperanza en su recinto.»
Y la esperanza dice quedamente
desde el reino sombrío:
«Vosotros me inventasteis, corazones.»
Y el corazón . . . :
«¡Dios mío!»

  El otoño ha dejado ya sin hojas
los álamos del río.
El agua ha adormecido en plata vieja
al polvo del camino.
Los gusanos se hunden soñolientos
en sus hogares fríos.
El águila se pierde en la montaña;
el viento dice: «Soy eterno ritmo.»
Se oyen las nanas a las cunas pobres,
y el llanto del rebaño en el aprisco.

  La mojada tristeza del paisaje
enseña como un libro
las arrugas severas que dejaron
los ojos pensadores de los siglos.

  Y mientras que descansan las estrellas
sobre el azul dormido,
mi corazón ve su ideal lejano
y pregunta:
«¡Dios mío!»
Pero, Dios mío, ¿a quién?
¿Quién es Dios mío?

shaking their heads pensively,
said: "The blue is unattainable.
When we were children we thought we'd reach it,
and we'd like to be like eagles
now that we've been wounded by the lightning.
The eagles own all the blue."
And the eagle in the distance:
"No, it isn't mine!
Because the blue is held by the stars
between their bright beams."
The stars: "We don't have it, either:
it's hidden somewhere above us."
And the dark distance: "The blue
is held by hope in its enclosure."
And hope says calmly
from its shady realm:
"Hearts, I'm an invention of yours."
And the heart . . . :
"O God!"

By now the autumn has left leafless
the poplars by the river.
The water has lulled to sleep, in the form of old silver,
the dust on the road.
The worms sink drowsily
into their cold homes.
The eagle is lost in the mountains;
the wind says: "I am eternal rhythm."
Lullabies are heard at humble cradles,
and the weeping of the flock in the fold.

The damp sadness of the landscape
shows like a book
the deep wrinkles left behind
by the pensive eyes of the centuries.

And while the stars rest
in the drowsy blue,
my heart sees its distant ideal
and asks:
"O God!"
But, God, whom does it ask?
Who is my God?

¿Por qué nuestra esperanza se adormece
y sentimos el fracaso lírico
y los ojos se cierran comprendiendo
todo el azul?

Sobre el paisaje viejo y el hogar humeante
quiero lanzar mi grito,
sollozando de mí como el gusano
deplora su destino.
Pidiendo lo del hombre: Amor inmenso
y azul como los álamos del río.
Azul de corazones y de fuerza,
el azul de mí mismo,
que me ponga en las manos la gran llave
que fuerce al infinito.
Sin terror y sin miedo ante la muerte,
escarchado de amor y de lirismo.
Aunque me hiera el rayo como al árbol
y me quede sin hojas y sin grito.

Ahora tengo en la frente rosas blancas
y la copa rebosando vino.

Aire de nocturno

1919

Tengo mucho miedo
de las hojas muertas,
miedo de los prados
llenos de rocío.
Yo voy a dormirme;
si no me despiertas,
dejaré a tu lado mi corazón frío.

«¿Qué es eso que suena
muy lejos?»
«Amor,
el viento en las vidrieras,
¡amor mío!»

Te puse collares
con gemas de aurora.
¿Por qué me abandonas

Why does our hope fall asleep,
and why do we feel a lyrical failure,
and why do our eyes close comprehending
all the blue?

Onto the old landscape and the smoking hearth
I want to hurl my cry,
sobbing over myself as the worm
deplores its destiny.
Asking for a man's lot: Love as immense
and blue as the poplars by the river.
Blueness of hearts and strength,
the blue of myself,
may it place in my hands the great key
that forces open infinity.
Without terror or fear of death,
frosted with love and lyricism.
Even if the lightning strikes me as it does the tree
and I remain without leaves and without a cry.

Now I have white roses on my brow
and a goblet brimming over with wine.

Melody of a Nocturne

1919

I have great fear
of dead leaves,
fear of meadows
full of dew.
I'm off to go to sleep;
if you don't awaken me,
I'll leave my cold heart beside you.

"What is that which resounds
so far away?"
"Love,
the wind against the window panes,
my love!"

I placed necklaces on you
with gems of dawn.
Why do you desert me

en este camino?
Si te vas muy lejos
mi pájaro llora
y la verde viña
no dará su vino.

«¿Qué es eso que suena
muy lejos?»
«Amor,
el viento en las vidrieras,
¡amor mío!»

Tú no sabrás nunca,
esfinge de nieve,
lo mucho que yo
te hubiera querido
esas madrugadas
cuando tanto llueve
y en la rama seca
se deshace el nido.

«¿Qué es eso que suena
muy lejos?»
«Amor,
el viento en las vidrieras,
¡amor mío!»

Nido

1919

¿Qué es lo que guardo en estos
momentos de tristeza?
¡Ay!, ¿quién tala mis bosques
dorados y floridos?
¿Qué leo en el espejo
de plata conmovida
que la aurora me ofrece
sobre el agua del río?
¿Qué gran olmo de idea
se ha tronchado en mi bosque?
¿Qué lluvia de silencio
me deja estremecido?

on this road?
If you go very far,
my bird will weep
and the green grapevine
won't give its wine.

    "What is that which resounds
so far away?"
"Love,
the wind against the window panes,
my love!"

    You will never know,
sphinx of snow,
how much I
would have loved you
in these early mornings
when it rains so much
and on the dry bough
the nest falls apart.

    "What is that which resounds
so far away?"
"Love,
the wind against the window panes,
my love!"

Nest

1919

    What is this that I'm holding onto in these
moments of sadness?
Ah! Who is felling my golden,
flowering forests?
What do I read in the mirror
of agitated silver
that the dawn presents to me
on the water of the river?
What great imaginary elm
has been broken in my forest?
What rain of silence
leaves me shaken?

Si a mi amor dejé muerto
en la ribera triste,
¿qué zarzales me ocultan
algo recién nacido?

Otra canción

1919 (Otoño)

¡El sueño se deshizo para siempre!

En la tarde lluviosa
mi corazón aprende
la tragedia otoñal
que los árboles llueven.

Y en la dulce tristeza
del paisaje que muere
mis voces se quebraron.
El sueño se deshizo para siempre.
¡Para siempre! ¡Dios mío!
Va cayendo la nieve
en el campo desierto
de mi vida,
y teme
la ilusión, que va lejos,
de helarse o de perderse.

¡Cómo me dice el agua
que el sueño se deshizo para siempre!
¿El sueño es infinito?
La niebla lo sostiene,
y la niebla es tan sólo
cansancio de la nieve.

Mi ritmo va contando
que el sueño se deshizo para siempre.
Y en la tarde brumosa
mi corazón aprende
la tragedia otoñal
que los árboles llueven.

If I left my love dead
on the sad riverbank,
what brambles are hiding from me
something newborn?

Another Song

1919 (Autumn)

The dream has dissolved forever!

In the rainy afternoon
my heart learns
the autumnal tragedy
that rains down from the trees.

And in the sweet sadness
of the dying landscape
my cries became hoarse.
The dream has dissolved forever.
Forever! O God!
The snow is falling
on the deserted field
of my life,
and my hopes,
which roam far, are afraid
of becoming frozen or lost.

How clearly the water tells me
that the dream has dissolved forever!
Is the dream infinite?
The mist sustains it,
and the mist is merely
the snow's weariness.

My rhythmic song is relating
that the dream has dissolved forever.
And in the foggy afternoon
my heart learns
the autumnal tragedy
that rains down from the trees.

El macho cabrío

1919

El rebaño de cabras ha pasado
junto al agua del río.
En la tarde de rosa y de zafiro,
llena de paz romántica,
yo miro
al gran macho cabrío.

¡Salve, demonio mudo!
Eres el más
intenso animal.
Místico eterno
del infierno
carnal . . .

¡Cuántos encantos
tiene tu barba,
tu frente ancha,
rudo don Juan!
¡Qué gran acento el de tu mirada
mefistofélica
y pasional!

Vas por los campos
con tu manada
hecho un eunuco
¡siendo un sultán!
Tu sed de sexo
nunca se apaga;
¡bien aprendiste
del padre Pan!

La cabra,
lenta te va siguiendo,
enamorada con humildad;
mas tus pasiones son insaciables;
Grecia vieja
te comprenderá.

¡Oh ser de hondas leyendas santas,
de ascetas flacos y Satanás
con piedras negras y cruces toscas,

The He-Goat

1919

The flock of goats has passed by
next to the waters of the river.
In the afternoon of rose and sapphire,
full of romantic peace,
I look at
the big billy-goat.

Hail, mute devil!
You are the most
intense animal.
An eternal mystic
of the fleshly
inferno . . .

How many charms
there are in your beard
and your wide forehead,
you coarse Don Juan!
What a loud cry there is your gaze,
Mephistophelian
and passionate!

You go through the fields
with your flock
as if you were a harem guard,
though really a sultan!
Your thirst for sex
is never quenched;
you were a good pupil
of father Pan!

The she-goat
follows you slowly,
in love but humble;
but your passions are insatiable;
ancient Greece
will understand you.

O you being of profound holy legends
about skinny ascetics and Satans
with black stones and crude crosses,

con fieras mansas y cuevas hondas
donde te vieron entre la sombra
soplar la llama
de lo sexual!

¡Machos cornudos
de bravas barbas!
¡Resumen negro a lo medieval!

Nacisteis juntos con Filomnedes
entre la espuma casta del mar,
y vuestras bocas
la acariciaron
bajo el asombro del mundo astral.

Sois de los bosques llenos de rosas
donde la luz es huracán;
sois de los prados de Anacreonte,
llenos con sangre de lo inmortal.

¡Machos cabríos!
Sois metamórfosis
de viejos sátiros
perdidos ya.
Vais derramando lujuria virgen
como no tuvo otro animal.

¡Illuminados del Mediodía!
Pararse en firme
para escuchar
que desde el fondo de las campiñas
el gallo os dice:
«¡Salud!», al pasar.

with tame wild beasts and deep caves
in which you were seen in the darkness
puffing up the flame
of sexuality!

Horned males
with wild beards!
A black summary of the Middle Ages!

You were born together with Philomnedes[14]
amid the chaste sea-foam,
and your lips
caressed her
as the astral world stood in awe.

You belong to the rose-filled forests
where light is a hurricane;
you belong to Anacreon's meadows,
filled with the blood of immortality.

He-goats!
You are the metamorphosis
of ancient satyrs
long lost.
You go about, spilling virginal lust
such as no other animal ever had.

Visionaries of the Noonday!
Remain still on solid ground
to hear
from the far reaches of the countryside
the rooster giving you
hearty greetings as you go by.

---

14. A variously interpreted term applied to Aphrodite in Hesiod's *Theogony,* and re-
curring nowhere else! Lorca was truly giving his readers a challenge at the very end of
his book!

Alphabetical List of Spanish Titles

Alphabetical List of Spanish First Lines

A CATALOG OF SELECTED
DOVER BOOKS
IN ALL FIELDS OF INTEREST

A CATALOG OF SELECTED DOVER

BOOKS IN ALL FIELDS OF INTEREST

CONCERNING THE SPIRITUAL IN ART, Wassily Kandinsky. Pioneering work by father of abstract art. Thoughts on color theory, nature of art. Analysis of earlier masters. 12 illustrations. 80pp. of text. 5⅜ x 8½.   23411-8

ANIMALS: 1,419 Copyright-Free Illustrations of Mammals, Birds, Fish, Insects, etc., Jim Harter (ed.). Clear wood engravings present, in extremely lifelike poses, over 1,000 species of animals. One of the most extensive pictorial sourcebooks of its kind. Captions. Index. 284pp. 9 x 12.   23766-4

CELTIC ART: The Methods of Construction, George Bain. Simple geometric techniques for making Celtic interlacements, spirals, Kells-type initials, animals, humans, etc. Over 500 illustrations. 160pp. 9 x 12. (Available in U.S. only.)   22923-8

AN ATLAS OF ANATOMY FOR ARTISTS, Fritz Schider. Most thorough reference work on art anatomy in the world. Hundreds of illustrations, including selections from works by Vesalius, Leonardo, Goya, Ingres, Michelangelo, others. 593 illustrations. 192pp. 7⅛ x 10¼.   20241-0

CELTIC HAND STROKE-BY-STROKE (Irish Half-Uncial from "The Book of Kells"): An Arthur Baker Calligraphy Manual, Arthur Baker. Complete guide to creating each letter of the alphabet in distinctive Celtic manner. Covers hand position, strokes, pens, inks, paper, more. Illustrated. 48pp. 8¼ x 11.   24336-2

EASY ORIGAMI, John Montroll. Charming collection of 32 projects (hat, cup, pelican, piano, swan, many more) specially designed for the novice origami hobbyist. Clearly illustrated easy-to-follow instructions insure that even beginning papercrafters will achieve successful results. 48pp. 8¼ x 11.   27298-2

THE COMPLETE BOOK OF BIRDHOUSE CONSTRUCTION FOR WOODWORKERS, Scott D. Campbell. Detailed instructions, illustrations, tables. Also data on bird habitat and instinct patterns. Bibliography. 3 tables. 63 illustrations in 15 figures. 48pp. 5¼ x 8½.   24407-5

BLOOMINGDALE'S ILLUSTRATED 1886 CATALOG: Fashions, Dry Goods and Housewares, Bloomingdale Brothers. Famed merchants' extremely rare catalog depicting about 1,700 products: clothing, housewares, firearms, dry goods, jewelry, more. Invaluable for dating, identifying vintage items. Also, copyright-free graphics for artists, designers. Co-published with Henry Ford Museum & Greenfield Village. 160pp. 8¼ x 11.   25780-0

HISTORIC COSTUME IN PICTURES, Braun & Schneider. Over 1,450 costumed figures in clearly detailed engravings–from dawn of civilization to end of 19th century. Captions. Many folk costumes. 256pp. 8⅜ x 11¾.   23150-X

STICKLEY CRAFTSMAN FURNITURE CATALOGS, Gustav Stickley and L. & J. G. Stickley. Beautiful, functional furniture in two authentic catalogs from 1910. 594 illustrations, including 277 photos, show settles, rockers, armchairs, reclining chairs, bookcases, desks, tables. 183pp. 6½ x 9¼. 23838-5

AMERICAN LOCOMOTIVES IN HISTORIC PHOTOGRAPHS: 1858 to 1949, Ron Ziel (ed.). A rare collection of 126 meticulously detailed official photographs, called "builder portraits," of American locomotives that majestically chronicle the rise of steam locomotive power in America. Introduction. Detailed captions. xi+ 129pp. 9 x 12. 27393-8

AMERICA'S LIGHTHOUSES: An Illustrated History, Francis Ross Holland, Jr. Delightfully written, profusely illustrated fact-filled survey of over 200 American lighthouses since 1716. History, anecdotes, technological advances, more. 240pp. 8 x 10¾. 25576-X

TOWARDS A NEW ARCHITECTURE, Le Corbusier. Pioneering manifesto by founder of "International School." Technical and aesthetic theories, views of industry, economics, relation of form to function, "mass-production split" and much more. Profusely illustrated. 320pp. 6⅛ x 9¼. (Available in U.S. only.) 25023-7

HOW THE OTHER HALF LIVES, Jacob Riis. Famous journalistic record, exposing poverty and degradation of New York slums around 1900, by major social reformer. 100 striking and influential photographs. 233pp. 10 x 7⅞. 22012-5

FRUIT KEY AND TWIG KEY TO TREES AND SHRUBS, William M. Harlow. One of the handiest and most widely used identification aids. Fruit key covers 120 deciduous and evergreen species; twig key 160 deciduous species. Easily used. Over 300 photographs. 126pp. 5⅜ x 8½. 20511-8

COMMON BIRD SONGS, Dr. Donald J. Borror. Songs of 60 most common U.S. birds: robins, sparrows, cardinals, bluejays, finches, more–arranged in order of increasing complexity. Up to 9 variations of songs of each species.
Cassette and manual 99911-4

ORCHIDS AS HOUSE PLANTS, Rebecca Tyson Northen. Grow cattleyas and many other kinds of orchids–in a window, in a case, or under artificial light. 63 illustrations. 148pp. 5⅜ x 8½. 23261-1

MONSTER MAZES, Dave Phillips. Masterful mazes at four levels of difficulty. Avoid deadly perils and evil creatures to find magical treasures. Solutions for all 32 exciting illustrated puzzles. 48pp. 8¼ x 11. 26005-4

MOZART'S DON GIOVANNI (DOVER OPERA LIBRETTO SERIES), Wolfgang Amadeus Mozart. Introduced and translated by Ellen H. Bleiler. Standard Italian libretto, with complete English translation. Convenient and thoroughly portable–an ideal companion for reading along with a recording or the performance itself. Introduction. List of characters. Plot summary. 121pp. 5¼ x 8½. 24944-1

TECHNICAL MANUAL AND DICTIONARY OF CLASSICAL BALLET, Gail Grant. Defines, explains, comments on steps, movements, poses and concepts. 15-page pictorial section. Basic book for student, viewer. 127pp. 5⅜ x 8½. 21843-0

THE CLARINET AND CLARINET PLAYING, David Pino. Lively, comprehensive work features suggestions about technique, musicianship, and musical interpretation, as well as guidelines for teaching, making your own reeds, and preparing for public performance. Includes an intriguing look at clarinet history. "A godsend," *The Clarinet,* Journal of the International Clarinet Society. Appendixes. 7 illus. 320pp. 5⅜ x 8½. 40270-3

HOLLYWOOD GLAMOR PORTRAITS, John Kobal (ed.). 145 photos from 1926-49. Harlow, Gable, Bogart, Bacall; 94 stars in all. Full background on photographers, technical aspects. 160pp. 8⅜ x 11¼. 23352-9

THE ANNOTATED CASEY AT THE BAT: A Collection of Ballads about the Mighty Casey/Third, Revised Edition, Martin Gardner (ed.). Amusing sequels and parodies of one of America's best-loved poems: Casey's Revenge, Why Casey Whiffed, Casey's Sister at the Bat, others. 256pp. 5⅜ x 8½. 28598-7

THE RAVEN AND OTHER FAVORITE POEMS, Edgar Allan Poe. Over 40 of the author's most memorable poems: "The Bells," "Ulalume," "Israfel," "To Helen," "The Conqueror Worm," "Eldorado," "Annabel Lee," many more. Alphabetic lists of titles and first lines. 64pp. 5 3/16 x 8¼. 26685-0

PERSONAL MEMOIRS OF U. S. GRANT, Ulysses Simpson Grant. Intelligent, deeply moving firsthand account of Civil War campaigns, considered by many the finest military memoirs ever written. Includes letters, historic photographs, maps and more. 528pp. 6⅛ x 9¼. 28587-1

ANCIENT EGYPTIAN MATERIALS AND INDUSTRIES, A. Lucas and J. Harris. Fascinating, comprehensive, thoroughly documented text describes this ancient civilization's vast resources and the processes that incorporated them in daily life, including the use of animal products, building materials, cosmetics, perfumes and incense, fibers, glazed ware, glass and its manufacture, materials used in the mummification process, and much more. 544pp. 6⅛ x 9¼. (Available in U.S. only.) 40446-3

RUSSIAN STORIES/RUSSKIE RASSKAZY: A Dual-Language Book, edited by Gleb Struve. Twelve tales by such masters as Chekhov, Tolstoy, Dostoevsky, Pushkin, others. Excellent word-for-word English translations on facing pages, plus teaching and study aids, Russian/English vocabulary, biographical/critical introductions, more. 416pp. 5⅜ x 8½. 26244-8

PHILADELPHIA THEN AND NOW: 60 Sites Photographed in the Past and Present, Kenneth Finkel and Susan Oyama. Rare photographs of City Hall, Logan Square, Independence Hall, Betsy Ross House, other landmarks juxtaposed with contemporary views. Captures changing face of historic city. Introduction. Captions. 128pp. 8¼ x 11. 25790-8

AIA ARCHITECTURAL GUIDE TO NASSAU AND SUFFOLK COUNTIES, LONG ISLAND, The American Institute of Architects, Long Island Chapter, and the Society for the Preservation of Long Island Antiquities. Comprehensive, well-researched and generously illustrated volume brings to life over three centuries of Long Island's great architectural heritage. More than 240 photographs with authoritative, extensively detailed captions. 176pp. 8¼ x 11. 26946-9

NORTH AMERICAN INDIAN LIFE: Customs and Traditions of 23 Tribes, Elsie Clews Parsons (ed.). 27 fictionalized essays by noted anthropologists examine religion, customs, government, additional facets of life among the Winnebago, Crow, Zuni, Eskimo, other tribes. 480pp. 6⅛ x 9¼. 27377-6

FRANK LLOYD WRIGHT'S DANA HOUSE, Donald Hoffmann. Pictorial essay of residential masterpiece with over 160 interior and exterior photos, plans, elevations, sketches and studies. 128pp. 9¼ x 10¾. 29120-0

THE MALE AND FEMALE FIGURE IN MOTION: 60 Classic Photographic Sequences, Eadweard Muybridge. 60 true-action photographs of men and women walking, running, climbing, bending, turning, etc., reproduced from rare 19th-century masterpiece. vi + 121pp. 9 x 12. 24745-7

1001 QUESTIONS ANSWERED ABOUT THE SEASHORE, N. J. Berrill and Jacquelyn Berrill. Queries answered about dolphins, sea snails, sponges, starfish, fishes, shore birds, many others. Covers appearance, breeding, growth, feeding, much more. 305pp. 5¼ x 8¼. 23366-9

ATTRACTING BIRDS TO YOUR YARD, William J. Weber. Easy-to-follow guide offers advice on how to attract the greatest diversity of birds: birdhouses, feeders, water and waterers, much more. 96pp. 5³⁄₁₆ x 8¼. 28927-3

MEDICINAL AND OTHER USES OF NORTH AMERICAN PLANTS: A Historical Survey with Special Reference to the Eastern Indian Tribes, Charlotte Erichsen-Brown. Chronological historical citations document 500 years of usage of plants, trees, shrubs native to eastern Canada, northeastern U.S. Also complete identifying information. 343 illustrations. 544pp. 6½ x 9¼. 25951-X

STORYBOOK MAZES, Dave Phillips. 23 stories and mazes on two-page spreads: Wizard of Oz, Treasure Island, Robin Hood, etc. Solutions. 64pp. 8¼ x 11. 23628-5

AMERICAN NEGRO SONGS: 230 Folk Songs and Spirituals, Religious and Secular, John W. Work. This authoritative study traces the African influences of songs sung and played by black Americans at work, in church, and as entertainment. The author discusses the lyric significance of such songs as "Swing Low, Sweet Chariot," "John Henry," and others and offers the words and music for 230 songs. Bibliography. Index of Song Titles. 272pp. 6½ x 9¼. 40271-1

MOVIE-STAR PORTRAITS OF THE FORTIES, John Kobal (ed.). 163 glamor, studio photos of 106 stars of the 1940s: Rita Hayworth, Ava Gardner, Marlon Brando, Clark Gable, many more. 176pp. 8⅜ x 11¼. 23546-7

BENCHLEY LOST AND FOUND, Robert Benchley. Finest humor from early 30s, about pet peeves, child psychologists, post office and others. Mostly unavailable elsewhere. 73 illustrations by Peter Arno and others. 183pp. 5⅜ x 8½. 22410-4

YEKL and THE IMPORTED BRIDEGROOM AND OTHER STORIES OF YIDDISH NEW YORK, Abraham Cahan. Film Hester Street based on *Yekl* (1896). Novel, other stories among first about Jewish immigrants on N.Y.'s East Side. 240pp. 5⅜ x 8½. 22427-9

SELECTED POEMS, Walt Whitman. Generous sampling from *Leaves of Grass*. Twenty-four poems include "I Hear America Singing," "Song of the Open Road," "I Sing the Body Electric," "When Lilacs Last in the Dooryard Bloom'd," "O Captain! My Captain!"—all reprinted from an authoritative edition. Lists of titles and first lines. 128pp. 5³⁄₁₆ x 8¼. 26878-0

THE BEST TALES OF HOFFMANN, E. T. A. Hoffmann. 10 of Hoffmann's most important stories: "Nutcracker and the King of Mice," "The Golden Flowerpot," etc. 458pp. 5⅜ x 8½. 21793-0

FROM FETISH TO GOD IN ANCIENT EGYPT, E. A. Wallis Budge. Rich detailed survey of Egyptian conception of "God" and gods, magic, cult of animals, Osiris, more. Also, superb English translations of hymns and legends. 240 illustrations. 545pp. 5⅜ x 8½. 25803-3

FRENCH STORIES/CONTES FRANÇAIS: A Dual-Language Book, Wallace Fowlie. Ten stories by French masters, Voltaire to Camus: "Micromegas" by Voltaire; "The Atheist's Mass" by Balzac; "Minuet" by de Maupassant; "The Guest" by Camus, six more. Excellent English translations on facing pages. Also French-English vocabulary list, exercises, more. 352pp. 5⅜ x 8½. 26443-2

CHICAGO AT THE TURN OF THE CENTURY IN PHOTOGRAPHS: 122 Historic Views from the Collections of the Chicago Historical Society, Larry A. Viskochil. Rare large-format prints offer detailed views of City Hall, State Street, the Loop, Hull House, Union Station, many other landmarks, circa 1904-1913. Introduction. Captions. Maps. 144pp. 9⅜ x 12¼. 24656-6

OLD BROOKLYN IN EARLY PHOTOGRAPHS, 1865-1929, William Lee Younger. Luna Park, Gravesend race track, construction of Grand Army Plaza, moving of Hotel Brighton, etc. 157 previously unpublished photographs. 165pp. 8⅞ x 11¾. 23587-4

THE MYTHS OF THE NORTH AMERICAN INDIANS, Lewis Spence. Rich anthology of the myths and legends of the Algonquins, Iroquois, Pawnees and Sioux, prefaced by an extensive historical and ethnological commentary. 36 illustrations. 480pp. 5⅜ x 8½. 25967-6

AN ENCYCLOPEDIA OF BATTLES: Accounts of Over 1,560 Battles from 1479 B.C. to the Present, David Eggenberger. Essential details of every major battle in recorded history from the first battle of Megiddo in 1479 B.C. to Grenada in 1984. List of Battle Maps. New Appendix covering the years 1967-1984. Index. 99 illustrations. 544pp. 6½ x 9¼. 24913-1

SAILING ALONE AROUND THE WORLD, Captain Joshua Slocum. First man to sail around the world, alone, in small boat. One of great feats of seamanship told in delightful manner. 67 illustrations. 294pp. 5⅜ x 8½. 20326-3

ANARCHISM AND OTHER ESSAYS, Emma Goldman. Powerful, penetrating, prophetic essays on direct action, role of minorities, prison reform, puritan hypocrisy, violence, etc. 271pp. 5⅜ x 8½. 22484-8

MYTHS OF THE HINDUS AND BUDDHISTS, Ananda K. Coomaraswamy and Sister Nivedita. Great stories of the epics; deeds of Krishna, Shiva, taken from puranas, Vedas, folk tales; etc. 32 illustrations. 400pp. 5⅜ x 8½. 21759-0

THE TRAUMA OF BIRTH, Otto Rank. Rank's controversial thesis that anxiety neurosis is caused by profound psychological trauma which occurs at birth. 256pp. 5⅜ x 8½. 27974-X

A THEOLOGICO-POLITICAL TREATISE, Benedict Spinoza. Also contains unfinished Political Treatise. Great classic on religious liberty, theory of government on common consent. R. Elwes translation. Total of 421pp. 5⅜ x 8½. 20249-6

MY BONDAGE AND MY FREEDOM, Frederick Douglass. Born a slave, Douglass became outspoken force in antislavery movement. The best of Douglass' autobiographies. Graphic description of slave life. 464pp. 5⅜ x 8½. 22457-0

FOLLOWING THE EQUATOR: A Journey Around the World, Mark Twain. Fascinating humorous account of 1897 voyage to Hawaii, Australia, India, New Zealand, etc. Ironic, bemused reports on peoples, customs, climate, flora and fauna, politics, much more. 197 illustrations. 720pp. 5⅜ x 8½. 26113-1

THE PEOPLE CALLED SHAKERS, Edward D. Andrews. Definitive study of Shakers: origins, beliefs, practices, dances, social organization, furniture and crafts, etc. 33 illustrations. 351pp. 5⅜ x 8½. 21081-2

THE MYTHS OF GREECE AND ROME, H. A. Guerber. A classic of mythology, generously illustrated, long prized for its simple, graphic, accurate retelling of the principal myths of Greece and Rome, and for its commentary on their origins and significance. With 64 illustrations by Michelangelo, Raphael, Titian, Rubens, Canova, Bernini and others. 480pp. 5⅜ x 8½. 27584-1

PSYCHOLOGY OF MUSIC, Carl E. Seashore. Classic work discusses music as a medium from psychological viewpoint. Clear treatment of physical acoustics, auditory apparatus, sound perception, development of musical skills, nature of musical feeling, host of other topics. 88 figures. 408pp. 5⅜ x 8½. 21851-1

THE PHILOSOPHY OF HISTORY, Georg W. Hegel. Great classic of Western thought develops concept that history is not chance but rational process, the evolution of freedom. 457pp. 5⅜ x 8½. 20112-0

THE BOOK OF TEA, Kakuzo Okakura. Minor classic of the Orient: entertaining, charming explanation, interpretation of traditional Japanese culture in terms of tea ceremony. 94pp. 5⅜ x 8½. 20070-1

LIFE IN ANCIENT EGYPT, Adolf Erman. Fullest, most thorough, detailed older account with much not in more recent books, domestic life, religion, magic, medicine, commerce, much more. Many illustrations reproduce tomb paintings, carvings, hieroglyphs, etc. 597pp. 5⅜ x 8½. 22632-8

SUNDIALS, Their Theory and Construction, Albert Waugh. Far and away the best, most thorough coverage of ideas, mathematics concerned, types, construction, adjusting anywhere. Simple, nontechnical treatment allows even children to build several of these dials. Over 100 illustrations. 230pp. 5⅜ x 8½. 22947-5

THEORETICAL HYDRODYNAMICS, L. M. Milne-Thomson. Classic exposition of the mathematical theory of fluid motion, applicable to both hydrodynamics and aerodynamics. Over 600 exercises. 768pp. 6⅛ x 9¼. 68970-0

SONGS OF EXPERIENCE: Facsimile Reproduction with 26 Plates in Full Color, William Blake. 26 full-color plates from a rare 1826 edition. Includes "The Tyger," "London," "Holy Thursday," and other poems. Printed text of poems. 48pp. 5¼ x 7. 24636-1

OLD-TIME VIGNETTES IN FULL COLOR, Carol Belanger Grafton (ed.). Over 390 charming, often sentimental illustrations, selected from archives of Victorian graphics—pretty women posing, children playing, food, flowers, kittens and puppies, smiling cherubs, birds and butterflies, much more. All copyright-free. 48pp. 9¼ x 12¼. 27269-9

PERSPECTIVE FOR ARTISTS, Rex Vicat Cole. Depth, perspective of sky and sea, shadows, much more, not usually covered. 391 diagrams, 81 reproductions of drawings and paintings. 279pp. 5⅜ x 8½. 22487-2

DRAWING THE LIVING FIGURE, Joseph Sheppard. Innovative approach to artistic anatomy focuses on specifics of surface anatomy, rather than muscles and bones. Over 170 drawings of live models in front, back and side views, and in widely varying poses. Accompanying diagrams. 177 illustrations. Introduction. Index. 144pp. 8⅜ x11¼. 26723-7

GOTHIC AND OLD ENGLISH ALPHABETS: 100 Complete Fonts, Dan X. Solo. Add power, elegance to posters, signs, other graphics with 100 stunning copyright-free alphabets: Blackstone, Dolbey, Germania, 97 more–including many lower-case, numerals, punctuation marks. 104pp. 8⅛ x 11. 24695-7

HOW TO DO BEADWORK, Mary White. Fundamental book on craft from simple projects to five-bead chains and woven works. 106 illustrations. 142pp. 5⅜ x 8. 20697-1

THE BOOK OF WOOD CARVING, Charles Marshall Sayers. Finest book for beginners discusses fundamentals and offers 34 designs. "Absolutely first rate . . . well thought out and well executed."–E. J. Tangerman. 118pp. 7¾ x 10⅝. 23654-4

ILLUSTRATED CATALOG OF CIVIL WAR MILITARY GOODS: Union Army Weapons, Insignia, Uniform Accessories, and Other Equipment, Schuyler, Hartley, and Graham. Rare, profusely illustrated 1846 catalog includes Union Army uniform and dress regulations, arms and ammunition, coats, insignia, flags, swords, rifles, etc. 226 illustrations. 160pp. 9 x 12. 24939-5

WOMEN'S FASHIONS OF THE EARLY 1900s: An Unabridged Republication of "New York Fashions, 1909," National Cloak & Suit Co. Rare catalog of mail-order fashions documents women's and children's clothing styles shortly after the turn of the century. Captions offer full descriptions, prices. Invaluable resource for fashion, costume historians. Approximately 725 illustrations. 128pp. 8⅜ x 11¼. 27276-1

THE 1912 AND 1915 GUSTAV STICKLEY FURNITURE CATALOGS, Gustav Stickley. With over 200 detailed illustrations and descriptions, these two catalogs are essential reading and reference materials and identification guides for Stickley furniture. Captions cite materials, dimensions and prices. 112pp. 6½ x 9¼. 26676-1

EARLY AMERICAN LOCOMOTIVES, John H. White, Jr. Finest locomotive engravings from early 19th century: historical (1804–74), main-line (after 1870), special, foreign, etc. 147 plates. 142pp. 11⅜ x 8¼. 22772-3

THE TALL SHIPS OF TODAY IN PHOTOGRAPHS, Frank O. Braynard. Lavishly illustrated tribute to nearly 100 majestic contemporary sailing vessels: Amerigo Vespucci, Clearwater, Constitution, Eagle, Mayflower, Sea Cloud, Victory, many more. Authoritative captions provide statistics, background on each ship. 190 black-and-white photographs and illustrations. Introduction. 128pp. 8⅞ x 11¾. 27163-3

LITTLE BOOK OF EARLY AMERICAN CRAFTS AND TRADES, Peter Stockham (ed.). 1807 children's book explains crafts and trades: baker, hatter, cooper, potter, and many others. 23 copperplate illustrations. 140pp. 4⅝ x 6.   23336-7

VICTORIAN FASHIONS AND COSTUMES FROM HARPER'S BAZAR, 1867–1898, Stella Blum (ed.). Day costumes, evening wear, sports clothes, shoes, hats, other accessories in over 1,000 detailed engravings. 320pp. 9⅜ x 12¼.   22990-4

GUSTAV STICKLEY, THE CRAFTSMAN, Mary Ann Smith. Superb study surveys broad scope of Stickley's achievement, especially in architecture. Design philosophy, rise and fall of the Craftsman empire, descriptions and floor plans for many Craftsman houses, more. 86 black-and-white halftones. 31 line illustrations. Introduction 208pp. 6½ x 9¼.   27210-9

THE LONG ISLAND RAIL ROAD IN EARLY PHOTOGRAPHS, Ron Ziel. Over 220 rare photos, informative text document origin (1844) and development of rail service on Long Island. Vintage views of early trains, locomotives, stations, passengers, crews, much more. Captions. 8⅞ x 11¾.   26301-0

VOYAGE OF THE LIBERDADE, Joshua Slocum. Great 19th-century mariner's thrilling, first-hand account of the wreck of his ship off South America, the 35-foot boat he built from the wreckage, and its remarkable voyage home. 128pp. 5⅜ x 8½.   40022-0

TEN BOOKS ON ARCHITECTURE, Vitruvius. The most important book ever written on architecture. Early Roman aesthetics, technology, classical orders, site selection, all other aspects. Morgan translation. 331pp. 5⅜ x 8½.   20645-9

THE HUMAN FIGURE IN MOTION, Eadweard Muybridge. More than 4,500 stopped-action photos, in action series, showing undraped men, women, children jumping, lying down, throwing, sitting, wrestling, carrying, etc. 390pp. 7⅞ x 10⅝.   20204-6 Clothbd.

TREES OF THE EASTERN AND CENTRAL UNITED STATES AND CANADA, William M. Harlow. Best one-volume guide to 140 trees. Full descriptions, woodlore, range, etc. Over 600 illustrations. Handy size. 288pp. 4½ x 6⅜.   20395-6

SONGS OF WESTERN BIRDS, Dr. Donald J. Borror. Complete song and call repertoire of 60 western species, including flycatchers, juncoes, cactus wrens, many more—includes fully illustrated booklet.   Cassette and manual 99913-0

GROWING AND USING HERBS AND SPICES, Milo Miloradovich. Versatile handbook provides all the information needed for cultivation and use of all the herbs and spices available in North America. 4 illustrations. Index. Glossary. 236pp. 5⅜ x 8½.   25058-X

BIG BOOK OF MAZES AND LABYRINTHS, Walter Shepherd. 50 mazes and labyrinths in all—classical, solid, ripple, and more—in one great volume. Perfect inexpensive puzzler for clever youngsters. Full solutions. 112pp. 8⅛ x 11.   22951-3

PIANO TUNING, J. Cree Fischer. Clearest, best book for beginner, amateur. Simple repairs, raising dropped notes, tuning by easy method of flattened fifths. No previous skills needed. 4 illustrations. 201pp. 5⅜ x 8½. 23267-0

HINTS TO SINGERS, Lillian Nordica. Selecting the right teacher, developing confidence, overcoming stage fright, and many other important skills receive thoughtful discussion in this indispensible guide, written by a world-famous diva of four decades' experience. 96pp. 5⅜ x 8½. 40094-8

THE COMPLETE NONSENSE OF EDWARD LEAR, Edward Lear. All nonsense limericks, zany alphabets, Owl and Pussycat, songs, nonsense botany, etc., illustrated by Lear. Total of 320pp. 5⅜ x 8½. (Available in U.S. only.) 20167-8

VICTORIAN PARLOUR POETRY: An Annotated Anthology, Michael R. Turner. 117 gems by Longfellow, Tennyson, Browning, many lesser-known poets. "The Village Blacksmith," "Curfew Must Not Ring Tonight," "Only a Baby Small," dozens more, often difficult to find elsewhere. Index of poets, titles, first lines. xxiii + 325pp. 5⅝ x 8¼. 27044-0

DUBLINERS, James Joyce. Fifteen stories offer vivid, tightly focused observations of the lives of Dublin's poorer classes. At least one, "The Dead," is considered a masterpiece. Reprinted complete and unabridged from standard edition. 160pp. 5³⁄₁₆ x 8¼. 26870-5

GREAT WEIRD TALES: 14 Stories by Lovecraft, Blackwood, Machen and Others, S. T. Joshi (ed.). 14 spellbinding tales, including "The Sin Eater," by Fiona McLeod, "The Eye Above the Mantel," by Frank Belknap Long, as well as renowned works by R. H. Barlow, Lord Dunsany, Arthur Machen, W. C. Morrow and eight other masters of the genre. 256pp. 5⅜ x 8½. (Available in U.S. only.) 40436-6

THE BOOK OF THE SACRED MAGIC OF ABRAMELIN THE MAGE, translated by S. MacGregor Mathers. Medieval manuscript of ceremonial magic. Basic document in Aleister Crowley, Golden Dawn groups. 268pp. 5⅜ x 8½. 23211-5

NEW RUSSIAN-ENGLISH AND ENGLISH-RUSSIAN DICTIONARY, M. A. O'Brien. This is a remarkably handy Russian dictionary, containing a surprising amount of information, including over 70,000 entries. 366pp. 4½ x 6⅛. 20208-9

HISTORIC HOMES OF THE AMERICAN PRESIDENTS, Second, Revised Edition, Irvin Haas. A traveler's guide to American Presidential homes, most open to the public, depicting and describing homes occupied by every American President from George Washington to George Bush. With visiting hours, admission charges, travel routes. 175 photographs. Index. 160pp. 8¼ x 11. 26751-2

NEW YORK IN THE FORTIES, Andreas Feininger. 162 brilliant photographs by the well-known photographer, formerly with *Life* magazine. Commuters, shoppers, Times Square at night, much else from city at its peak. Captions by John von Hartz. 181pp. 9¼ x 10¾. 23585-8

INDIAN SIGN LANGUAGE, William Tomkins. Over 525 signs developed by Sioux and other tribes. Written instructions and diagrams. Also 290 pictographs. 111pp. 6⅛ x 9¼. 22029-X

CATALOG OF DOVER BOOKS

ANATOMY: A Complete Guide for Artists, Joseph Sheppard. A master of figure drawing shows artists how to render human anatomy convincingly. Over 460 illustrations. 224pp. 8⅜ x 11¼. 27279-6

MEDIEVAL CALLIGRAPHY: Its History and Technique, Marc Drogin. Spirited history, comprehensive instruction manual covers 13 styles (ca. 4th century through 15th). Excellent photographs; directions for duplicating medieval techniques with modern tools. 224pp. 8⅜ x 11¼. 26142-5

DRIED FLOWERS: How to Prepare Them, Sarah Whitlock and Martha Rankin. Complete instructions on how to use silica gel, meal and borax, perlite aggregate, sand and borax, glycerine and water to create attractive permanent flower arrangements. 12 illustrations. 32pp. 5⅜ x 8½. 21802-3

EASY-TO-MAKE BIRD FEEDERS FOR WOODWORKERS, Scott D. Campbell. Detailed, simple-to-use guide for designing, constructing, caring for and using feeders. Text, illustrations for 12 classic and contemporary designs. 96pp. 5⅜ x 8½. 25847-5

SCOTTISH WONDER TALES FROM MYTH AND LEGEND, Donald A. Mackenzie. 16 lively tales tell of giants rumbling down mountainsides, of a magic wand that turns stone pillars into warriors, of gods and goddesses, evil hags, powerful forces and more. 240pp. 5⅜ x 8½. 29677-6

THE HISTORY OF UNDERCLOTHES, C. Willett Cunnington and Phyllis Cunnington. Fascinating, well-documented survey covering six centuries of English undergarments, enhanced with over 100 illustrations: 12th-century laced-up bodice, footed long drawers (1795), 19th-century bustles, 19th-century corsets for men, Victorian "bust improvers," much more. 272pp. 5⅝ x 8¼. 27124-2

ARTS AND CRAFTS FURNITURE: The Complete Brooks Catalog of 1912, Brooks Manufacturing Co. Photos and detailed descriptions of more than 150 now very collectible furniture designs from the Arts and Crafts movement depict davenports, settees, buffets, desks, tables, chairs, bedsteads, dressers and more, all built of solid, quarter-sawed oak. Invaluable for students and enthusiasts of antiques, Americana and the decorative arts. 80pp. 6½ x 9¼. 27471-3

WILBUR AND ORVILLE: A Biography of the Wright Brothers, Fred Howard. Definitive, crisply written study tells the full story of the brothers' lives and work. A vividly written biography, unparalleled in scope and color, that also captures the spirit of an extraordinary era. 560pp. 6⅛ x 9¼. 40297-5

THE ARTS OF THE SAILOR: Knotting, Splicing and Ropework, Hervey Garrett Smith. Indispensable shipboard reference covers tools, basic knots and useful hitches; handsewing and canvas work, more. Over 100 illustrations. Delightful reading for sea lovers. 256pp. 5⅜ x 8½. 26440-8

FRANK LLOYD WRIGHT'S FALLINGWATER: The House and Its History, Second, Revised Edition, Donald Hoffmann. A total revision–both in text and illustrations–of the standard document on Fallingwater, the boldest, most personal architectural statement of Wright's mature years, updated with valuable new material from the recently opened Frank Lloyd Wright Archives. "Fascinating"–*The New York Times*. 116 illustrations. 128pp. 9¼ x 10¾. 27430-6

PHOTOGRAPHIC SKETCHBOOK OF THE CIVIL WAR, Alexander Gardner. 100 photos taken on field during the Civil War. Famous shots of Manassas Harper's Ferry, Lincoln, Richmond, slave pens, etc. 244pp. 10⅝ x 8¼. 22731-6

FIVE ACRES AND INDEPENDENCE, Maurice G. Kains. Great back-to-the-land classic explains basics of self-sufficient farming. The one book to get. 95 illustrations. 397pp. 5⅜ x 8½. 20974-1

SONGS OF EASTERN BIRDS, Dr. Donald J. Borror. Songs and calls of 60 species most common to eastern U.S.: warblers, woodpeckers, flycatchers, thrushes, larks, many more in high-quality recording. Cassette and manual 99912-2

A MODERN HERBAL, Margaret Grieve. Much the fullest, most exact, most useful compilation of herbal material. Gigantic alphabetical encyclopedia, from aconite to zedoary, gives botanical information, medical properties, folklore, economic uses, much else. Indispensable to serious reader. 161 illustrations. 888pp. 6½ x 9¼. 2-vol. set. (Available in U.S. only.) Vol. I: 22798-7
Vol. II: 22799-5

HIDDEN TREASURE MAZE BOOK, Dave Phillips. Solve 34 challenging mazes accompanied by heroic tales of adventure. Evil dragons, people-eating plants, blood-thirsty giants, many more dangerous adversaries lurk at every twist and turn. 34 mazes, stories, solutions. 48pp. 8¼ x 11. 24566-7

LETTERS OF W. A. MOZART, Wolfgang A. Mozart. Remarkable letters show bawdy wit, humor, imagination, musical insights, contemporary musical world; includes some letters from Leopold Mozart. 276pp. 5⅜ x 8½. 22859-2

BASIC PRINCIPLES OF CLASSICAL BALLET, Agrippina Vaganova. Great Russian theoretician, teacher explains methods for teaching classical ballet. 118 illus-trations. 175pp. 5⅜ x 8½. 22036-2

THE JUMPING FROG, Mark Twain. Revenge edition. The original story of The Celebrated Jumping Frog of Calaveras County, a hapless French translation, and Twain's hilarious "retranslation" from the French. 12 illustrations. 66pp. 5⅜ x 8½.
22686-7

BEST REMEMBERED POEMS, Martin Gardner (ed.). The 126 poems in this superb collection of 19th- and 20th-century British and American verse range from Shelley's "To a Skylark" to the impassioned "Renascence" of Edna St. Vincent Millay and to Edward Lear's whimsical "The Owl and the Pussycat." 224pp. 5⅜ x 8½.
27165-X

COMPLETE SONNETS, William Shakespeare. Over 150 exquisite poems deal with love, friendship, the tyranny of time, beauty's evanescence, death and other themes in language of remarkable power, precision and beauty. Glossary of archaic terms. 80pp. 5³⁄₁₆ x 8¼. 26686-9

THE BATTLES THAT CHANGED HISTORY, Fletcher Pratt. Eminent historian profiles 16 crucial conflicts, ancient to modern, that changed the course of civiliza-tion. 352pp. 5⅜ x 8½. 41129-X

THE WIT AND HUMOR OF OSCAR WILDE, Alvin Redman (ed.). More than 1,000 ripostes, paradoxes, wisecracks: Work is the curse of the drinking classes; I can resist everything except temptation; etc. 258pp. 5⅜ x 8½. 20602-5

SHAKESPEARE LEXICON AND QUOTATION DICTIONARY, Alexander Schmidt. Full definitions, locations, shades of meaning in every word in plays and poems. More than 50,000 exact quotations. 1,485pp. 6½ x 9¼. 2-vol. set.
Vol. 1: 22726-X
Vol. 2: 22727-8

SELECTED POEMS, Emily Dickinson. Over 100 best-known, best-loved poems by one of America's foremost poets, reprinted from authoritative early editions. No comparable edition at this price. Index of first lines. 64pp. 5³⁄₁₆ x 8¼. 26466-1

THE INSIDIOUS DR. FU-MANCHU, Sax Rohmer. The first of the popular mystery series introduces a pair of English detectives to their archnemesis, the diabolical Dr. Fu-Manchu. Flavorful atmosphere, fast-paced action, and colorful characters enliven this classic of the genre. 208pp. 5³⁄₁₆ x 8¼. 29898-1

THE MALLEUS MALEFICARUM OF KRAMER AND SPRENGER, translated by Montague Summers. Full text of most important witchhunter's "bible," used by both Catholics and Protestants. 278pp. 6⅝ x 10. 22802-9

SPANISH STORIES/CUENTOS ESPAÑOLES: A Dual-Language Book, Angel Flores (ed.). Unique format offers 13 great stories in Spanish by Cervantes, Borges, others. Faithful English translations on facing pages. 352pp. 5⅜ x 8½. 25399-6

GARDEN CITY, LONG ISLAND, IN EARLY PHOTOGRAPHS, 1869–1919, Mildred H. Smith. Handsome treasury of 118 vintage pictures, accompanied by carefully researched captions, document the Garden City Hotel fire (1899), the Vanderbilt Cup Race (1908), the first airmail flight departing from the Nassau Boulevard Aerodrome (1911), and much more. 96pp. 8⅞ x 11¾. 40669-5

OLD QUEENS, N.Y., IN EARLY PHOTOGRAPHS, Vincent F. Seyfried and William Asadorian. Over 160 rare photographs of Maspeth, Jamaica, Jackson Heights, and other areas. Vintage views of DeWitt Clinton mansion, 1939 World's Fair and more. Captions. 192pp. 8⅞ x 11. 26358-4

CAPTURED BY THE INDIANS: 15 Firsthand Accounts, 1750-1870, Frederick Drimmer. Astounding true historical accounts of grisly torture, bloody conflicts, relentless pursuits, miraculous escapes and more, by people who lived to tell the tale. 384pp. 5⅜ x 8½. 24901-8

THE WORLD'S GREAT SPEECHES (Fourth Enlarged Edition), Lewis Copeland, Lawrence W. Lamm, and Stephen J. McKenna. Nearly 300 speeches provide public speakers with a wealth of updated quotes and inspiration–from Pericles' funeral oration and William Jennings Bryan's "Cross of Gold Speech" to Malcolm X's powerful words on the Black Revolution and Earl of Spenser's tribute to his sister, Diana, Princess of Wales. 944pp. 5⅜ x 8⅜. 40903-1

THE BOOK OF THE SWORD, Sir Richard F. Burton. Great Victorian scholar/adventurer's eloquent, erudite history of the "queen of weapons"–from prehistory to early Roman Empire. Evolution and development of early swords, variations (sabre, broadsword, cutlass, scimitar, etc.), much more. 336pp. 6⅛ x 9¼.
25434-8

AUTOBIOGRAPHY: The Story of My Experiments with Truth, Mohandas K. Gandhi. Boyhood, legal studies, purification, the growth of the Satyagraha (nonviolent protest) movement. Critical, inspiring work of the man responsible for the freedom of India. 480pp. 5⅜ x 8½. (Available in U.S. only.) 24593-4

CELTIC MYTHS AND LEGENDS, T. W. Rolleston. Masterful retelling of Irish and Welsh stories and tales. Cuchulain, King Arthur, Deirdre, the Grail, many more. First paperback edition. 58 full-page illustrations. 512pp. 5⅜ x 8½. 26507-2

THE PRINCIPLES OF PSYCHOLOGY, William James. Famous long course complete, unabridged. Stream of thought, time perception, memory, experimental methods; great work decades ahead of its time. 94 figures. 1,391pp. 5⅜ x 8½. 2-vol. set. Vol. I: 20381-6 Vol. II: 20382-4

THE WORLD AS WILL AND REPRESENTATION, Arthur Schopenhauer. Definitive English translation of Schopenhauer's life work, correcting more than 1,000 errors, omissions in earlier translations. Translated by E. F. J. Payne. Total of 1,269pp. 5⅜ x 8½. 2-vol. set. Vol. 1: 21761-2 Vol. 2: 21762-0

MAGIC AND MYSTERY IN TIBET, Madame Alexandra David-Neel. Experiences among lamas, magicians, sages, sorcerers, Bonpa wizards. A true psychic discovery. 32 illustrations. 321pp. 5⅜ x 8½. (Available in U.S. only.) 22682-4

THE EGYPTIAN BOOK OF THE DEAD, E. A. Wallis Budge. Complete reproduction of Ani's papyrus, finest ever found. Full hieroglyphic text, interlinear transliteration, word-for-word translation, smooth translation. 533pp. 6½ x 9¼. 21866-X

MATHEMATICS FOR THE NONMATHEMATICIAN, Morris Kline. Detailed, college-level treatment of mathematics in cultural and historical context, with numerous exercises. Recommended Reading Lists. Tables. Numerous figures. 641pp. 5⅜ x 8½. 24823-2

PROBABILISTIC METHODS IN THE THEORY OF STRUCTURES, Isaac Elishakoff. Well-written introduction covers the elements of the theory of probability from two or more random variables, the reliability of such multivariable structures, the theory of random function, Monte Carlo methods of treating problems incapable of exact solution, and more. Examples. 502pp. 5⅜ x 8½. 40691-1

THE RIME OF THE ANCIENT MARINER, Gustave Doré, S. T. Coleridge. Doré's finest work; 34 plates capture moods, subtleties of poem. Flawless full-size reproductions printed on facing pages with authoritative text of poem. "Beautiful. Simply beautiful."–*Publisher's Weekly.* 77pp. 9¼ x 12. 22305-1

NORTH AMERICAN INDIAN DESIGNS FOR ARTISTS AND CRAFTSPEOPLE, Eva Wilson. Over 360 authentic copyright-free designs adapted from Navajo blankets, Hopi pottery, Sioux buffalo hides, more. Geometrics, symbolic figures, plant and animal motifs, etc. 128pp. 8⅜ x 11. (Not for sale in the United Kingdom.) 25341-4

SCULPTURE: Principles and Practice, Louis Slobodkin. Step-by-step approach to clay, plaster, metals, stone; classical and modern. 253 drawings, photos. 255pp. 8⅛ x 11. 22960-2

THE INFLUENCE OF SEA POWER UPON HISTORY, 1660–1783, A. T. Mahan. Influential classic of naval history and tactics still used as text in war colleges. First paperback edition. 4 maps. 24 battle plans. 640pp. 5⅜ x 8½. 25509-3

CANBY PUBLIC LIBRARY
292 N. HOLLY

THE STORY OF THE TITANIC AS TOLD BY ITS SURVIVORS, Jack Winocour (ed.). What it was really like. Panic, despair, shocking inefficiency, and a little heroism. More thrilling than any fictional account. 26 illustrations. 320pp. 5⅜ x 8½.
20610-6

FAIRY AND FOLK TALES OF THE IRISH PEASANTRY, William Butler Yeats (ed.). Treasury of 64 tales from the twilight world of Celtic myth and legend: "The Soul Cages," "The Kildare Pooka," "King O'Toole and his Goose," many more. Introduction and Notes by W. B. Yeats. 352pp. 5⅜ x 8½.
26941-8

BUDDHIST MAHAYANA TEXTS, E. B. Cowell and others (eds.). Superb, accurate translations of basic documents in Mahayana Buddhism, highly important in history of religions. The Buddha-karita of Asvaghosha, Larger Sukhavativyuha, more. 448pp. 5⅜ x 8½.
25552-2

ONE TWO THREE . . . INFINITY: Facts and Speculations of Science, George Gamow. Great physicist's fascinating, readable overview of contemporary science: number theory, relativity, fourth dimension, entropy, genes, atomic structure, much more. 128 illustrations. Index. 352pp. 5⅜ x 8½.
25664-2

EXPERIMENTATION AND MEASUREMENT, W. J. Youden. Introductory manual explains laws of measurement in simple terms and offers tips for achieving accuracy and minimizing errors. Mathematics of measurement, use of instruments, experimenting with machines. 1994 edition. Foreword. Preface. Introduction. Epilogue. Selected Readings. Glossary. Index. Tables and figures. 128pp. 5⅜ x 8½. 40451-X

DALÍ ON MODERN ART: The Cuckolds of Antiquated Modern Art, Salvador Dalí. Influential painter skewers modern art and its practitioners. Outrageous evaluations of Picasso, Cézanne, Turner, more. 15 renderings of paintings discussed. 44 calligraphic decorations by Dalí. 96pp. 5⅜ x 8½. (Available in U.S. only.)
29220-7

ANTIQUE PLAYING CARDS: A Pictorial History, Henry René D'Allemagne. Over 900 elaborate, decorative images from rare playing cards (14th–20th centuries): Bacchus, death, dancing dogs, hunting scenes, royal coats of arms, players cheating, much more. 96pp. 9¼ x 12¼.
29265-7

MAKING FURNITURE MASTERPIECES: 30 Projects with Measured Drawings, Franklin H. Gottshall. Step-by-step instructions, illustrations for constructing handsome, useful pieces, among them a Sheraton desk, Chippendale chair, Spanish desk, Queen Anne table and a William and Mary dressing mirror. 224pp. 8⅛ x 11¼.
29338-6

THE FOSSIL BOOK: A Record of Prehistoric Life, Patricia V. Rich et al. Profusely illustrated definitive guide covers everything from single-celled organisms and dinosaurs to birds and mammals and the interplay between climate and man. Over 1,500 illustrations. 760pp. 7½ x 10⅛.
29371-8

Paperbound unless otherwise indicated. Available at your book dealer, online at **www.doverpublications.com**, or by writing to Dept. GI, Dover Publications, Inc., 31 East 2nd Street, Mineola, NY 11501. For current price information or for free catalogues (please indicate field of interest), write to Dover Publications or log on to **www.doverpublications.com** and see every Dover book in print. Dover publishes more than 500 books each year on science, elementary and advanced mathematics, biology, music, art, literary history, social sciences, and other areas.

CANBY PUBLIC LIBRARY
292 N. HOLLY
CANBY, OR 97013